New Worlds
Year One

ALSO BY MARIE BRENNAN

The Memoirs of Lady Trent
A Natural History of Dragons
The Tropic of Serpents
Voyage of the Basilisk
In the Labyrinth of Drakes
Within the Sanctuary of Wings

Onyx Court
Midnight Never Come
Deeds of Men
In Ashes Lie
A Star Shall Fall
With Fate Conspire

Wilders
Lies and Prophecy
Chains and Memory

Doppelganger
Warrior
Witch

Collections
Ars Historica
Maps to Nowhere
Monstrous Beauty

Nonfiction
Writing Fight Scenes
Dice Tales

New Worlds Year One

A Writer's Guide to the Art of Worldbuilding

Marie Brennan

NEW WORLDS, YEAR ONE
Copyright © 2018 by Marie Brennan
All Rights Reserved, including the right to reproduce this book or portions thereof in any form.

First published 2018 by Book View Café Publishing Cooperative
P.O. Box 1624
Cedar Crest, NM 87008-1624
www.bookviewcafe.com

Print edition 2018
ISBN: 978-1-61138-747-6

Cover by Pati Nagle from photo by msandersmusic
Interior design by Marissa Doyle

Table of Contents

Introduction 1
The Shape of the World 5
Plate Tectonics 9
Rivers 13
Mountains 17
Deserts 21
Natural Disasters 25
How Many Seasons? 29
Measuring Time 33
Where Does the Food Come From? 37
Local and Imported Food 41
Kitchens 45
Dining Customs 49
Phonology the Easy Way 53
What's in a Name? 57
Names and Their Meaning 61
The Etiquette of Names 65
Greetings and Respect 69
Gestures of Contempt 73
Insults 77
Profanity 81
Idioms and Slang 85

Folk Magic 89
Lucky Charms 93
Curse You! 97
Divination 101
Birthdays 105
Childhood 109
Respect Your Elders 113
Rites of Passage 117
Lineage 121
Third Cousin Twice Removed 125
Fictive Kinship 129
Residence Patterns 133
Marriage 137
Structures of Marriage 141
Buying and Selling Spouses 145
Divorce 149
Funerary Customs 153
Cannibalism 157
Mourning 161
The Afterlife 165
Your Money's Worth 169
Follow the Money 173
All that Glitters Is Not Gold 177
Signs of Power 181
Sumptuary Laws 185
Status Without Wealth 189
The History We Live In 193
Worldbuilding as a Habit of Thought 197
Bricolage 201
Liminality 205
Afterword 209

Introduction

Every time I've thought about trying to write a book on science fiction and fantasy worldbuilding, I've run aground on the sheer size of the topic.

When you stop to look at the world we live in, it's fractally complex: a relatively simple-sounding facet of culture like "marriage" unpacks to the question of who gets married, and in what combinations, and why, and how, and how long does it last, and how can it end, and what happens after it ends, and of course all those questions have multiple answers because they're handled differently in different societies at different times in history. Marriage among the pre-contact Lakota is not the same as marriage among nineteenth-century Italian Catholic peasants is not the same as marriage among Tang Dynasty Chinese aristocrats.

You can lose yourself forever on that single word, "marriage"—and that's before you even get to all the concepts tied into it, like lineage and residence patterns and inheritance. The toe bone's connected to the foot bone, the art bone's connected to the religion bone, and so on until you have a body the size of an entire world. How can I discuss something that sprawling and huge?

Enter Patreon.

Without Patreon, this book would probably not exist. Because the only way to tackle a subject as complex as worldbuilding is piecemeal over a long period of time—a format ideally suited to something like a blog series, but that requires a lot of time and effort. The subscription format Patreon offers made it possible for me to justify putting in the work necessary to do justice to the idea of worldbuilding. So if you have purchased this book, please take a moment to thank my patrons, and consider becoming one yourself!

With that out of the way: who am I, and why am I putting out a sixty-thousand-word book on worldbuilding that says "Year One" on the cover, implying there will be more to come?

I'm a fantasy author, but the main reason I'm doing this is that I am, or at least used to be, an anthropologist. My undergraduate degree is in archaeology and folklore; I finished graduate coursework in cultural anthropology and folklore before leaving school to write full-time. My whole life, my interest has been in history, foreign cultures, mythology, anything that introduces me to different ways of thinking and living. And because I never settled down to any one specific place or period to the exclusion of others, my head is packed full of everything from Classic Mayan civilization to the Japanese Sengoku period to Viking Age Scandinavia.

As you might expect, this spills over to my fiction. When people ask whether my story ideas start with a character or a plot, I usually say "a world." Not in the sense that I have the whole setting in my mind, but rather in the sense that I can't separate the character or the plot from the world they live in: the protagonist is a certain kind of person because they live in a certain kind of society, or a conflict crops up because of something about how the culture works. My very favorite kinds of stories are the ones where those things are so intertwined that trying to transplant the story to another setting simply wouldn't work.

Digging into the chewy little details of a society can provide you with interesting new conflicts or fresh ways to approach old conflicts. In some cases this will become the centerpiece of your story; in others you merely slip it into the background, adding a bit of flavor that makes the reader feel you've transported them to another world.

It's true that every piece of fiction includes some worldbuilding, however minor; if it didn't, we'd call it nonfiction. Writers of mainstream literary fiction make up towns. Or they set something in a real town but an imaginary neighborhood. Or the neighborhood is real, but the local coffee shop the protagonist frequents isn't. Even if I set a story in my hometown, on the street I grew up on, in the house I lived in for eighteen years, and put my protagonist in my old bedroom, I'd still have to make decisions about what's in that room, and how it changes as the story goes along.

But the main focus of this book is on worlds far more different from our own: the secondary worlds of fantasy, the familiar-but-not timelines of alternate history, or the other planets of space-traveling science fiction. Even if you're writing urban fantasy or near-future science fiction, there's still the question of how the magic or the invented technology works, how it affects society, what cultural tics have built up around it (like slang or new superstitions), and so on. The more you diverge from current reality, the wider the scope of your potential changes gets...until at the far end of the spectrum, pretty much *everything* is up for grabs.

And I do mean everything. If the world you're writing about is not our own in any time period or alternate track of history, then who's to say anything is the same? You might have adar and kimmet and renitin trees instead of oaks and maples and birches. Or maybe the closest analogue to our concept of "tree" is an ambulatory organism made of living crystal. In your invented world, the very ground the characters walk on might be a woven textile they have to maintain or they'll fall into an abyss. Maybe gravity changes direction based on the phase of the moon. Maybe electromagnetism doesn't work at all. OH MY GOD, WHERE DOES IT END?

It ends where you want it to—which for most of us is going to be long before we get to the point of throwing electromagnetism out the window. A portion of this book addresses the natural environment, but its focus is far more on the cultural end of things, the institutions and practices human beings have invented to organize themselves. I give a wide variety of examples where I can, especially trying to draw on sources that are less likely to be familiar to readers living in modern Western industrialized societies—because there's no reason speculative fiction should limit itself to such a narrow slice of possibility.

This book collects the first year's worth of the New World Patreon, from March 2017 through February 2018. It is not, however, in original posting order: I've rearranged them to flow more logically from one to the next, since you're likely to be reading them more rapidly than one essay per week. In rough terms, they go from the natural world, to food and its customs, to phonology and names, to etiquette, to folk magic, to stages of life, to kinship and marriage, to funerary practices, to money and wealth.

The final three pieces are a little different. One of the funding goals for the Patreon is a bonus "theory" essay in the months that have five Fridays (the basic setup being four posts a month). Instead of addressing specific cultural practices, these posts look at the ways writers approach worldbuilding, and various under-pinning concepts you can use to add power to the settings you create.

The promise implicit in the title—*New Worlds, Year One*—is an accurate one. As of the publication of this book, the Patreon is still going strong. Right now there are fifty-eight items on my list of additional topics to cover, and I add new things faster than I write posts. There will be a Year Two for certain, and a Year Three is very likely. But for now, twelve months' worth of posts is enough to start with. Enjoy your journey, and may it give you much inspiration for your own work!

—Marie Brennan
San Mateo, California

The Shape of the World

I've been re-reading the comic book series *Elfquest*, the setting of which is usually referred to as the World of Two Moons—for the very simple and obvious reason that there are two moons in the sky.

This is surprisingly rare in fantasy.

Science fiction, sure. Having multiple moons in the sky, or multiple suns, or planetary rings, can be a quick and easy way to signal "alien world" to the reader. But in fantasy it's almost always just one sun and one moon, lighting a world that is either spherical or unspecified in shape. I can name a few exceptions, of course. Terry Pratchett's Discworld is famously named for the fact that it really is a flat disc sitting atop the backs of four elephants which themselves stand on the back of the great turtle A'Tuin, who swims through the void of space. *Voyage of the Dawn Treader*, the third book of the Chronicles of Narnia, features the protagonists sailing to the eastern edge of what appears to be a flat world. And in Elizabeth Bear's Eternal Sky trilogy, the contents of the heavens depend on whose territory you're in; cross a border (or get conquered), and the sky can change completely. I'm sure there are others, too. But by and large, this isn't an aspect of the world that most fantasy writers bother to fiddle with.

Why not?

I can think of two reasons, coming at the situation from opposite directions. (Well, three—the third being that it never even occurs to the author to play around with this aspect of their setting.) First, some writers feel they would have to address the scientific underpinnings and consequences of making such a change. Taking two moons as an example: what does that do to the tides? Can you have rings around an Earth-like planet, or does that only happen with a gas giant? Etc. When you're writing planetary science fiction, there's more likely to be a general expectation that you should get those details right, and not everyone will want to go to that extra level of work. And since we all have things we get hung up on, a fantasy writer may likewise feel that they should pay attention to the science...even though nothing says your invented world *has* to behave the same way. If the bands across the sky are not an astronomical phenomenon but rather the shattered remains of the gods' enemies, the land they arch over can take any form you like. If tides are caused by the yearning of the sea goddess to return to the land that rejected her, then what does it matter how many moons are in the sky? Heck, your story may not even take place in a coastal location where the behavior of the tides will matter.

This brings us to our second possible reason, which is that the writer may not see the point of messing around with basic world-shape elements. From this perspective, if your whole novel takes place in a single city, then whether the world is a round ball or a flat disc or something else is (at least theoretically) irrelevant to the story. Having multiple moons would at most be a throwaway detail. Planetary rings, or something that looks like them, are one more thing you have to describe to the reader, which may distract them from the plot and setting elements that have real impact on the story.

Your mileage may vary, but I'm a fan of throwaway details, those little side notes that give the setting flavor without being load-bearing. Especially because everything in the setting is interconnected: even if the shape of the place isn't directly tied into your plot, it will still affect the way the characters live and speak. In *Elfquest* the main characters refer to the two moons as the Mother Moon and the Child Moon; you'd get a different vibe if they were instead called the Hunter Moon and the Prey Moon, or the King Moon and Peasant Moon. So even a passing line about "the moons were thin crescents, and the Hunter Moon had almost caught the Prey Moon" adds color to the setting—a very different color than you'd get if instead "the moons were thin crescents, and the Mother Moon was cradling the Child Moon in her arms." Speech will reflect these basic details: people may not use phrases like "around the world" if their world isn't a globe. If their creation story follows the "emergence" pattern like the ones common in the American Southwest, with humans climbing up through a series of different worlds before settling into this one, that could be reflected in everything from architecture (the small hole in the floor of an underground kiva represents the portal they came through) to their annual festivals. If you're writing very epic fantasy, your characters might go back down through that hole to the world below—but even if they don't, those beliefs will still shape everything around them.

I'd love to see more fantasy authors play around with these fundamental structures. Give me multiple suns, multiple moons, planetary rings or something that looks a lot like them. Give me flat worlds. Give me worlds that are round balls—with everyone living on the *inside* of that ball, and the sun stationary in the center. Give me worlds that are long interlaced bands, and you can leap across the gap between one part of the band and another if you know what you're doing. Give me suns that are fiery chariots being driven across the sky, and then dangerous underworlds they have to traverse before they can bring the next dawn. Give me moons that literally are eaten by the darkness and then re-emerge, having temporarily defeated their foe. Because if you're writing fantasy, *there's no reason that can't be true.* No reason you can't take the ideas of mythology and treat them as the actual, functional reality of the setting, with all the consequences that implies. Richard Garfinkle did this brilliantly in *Celestial Matters*, where Ptolemaic astronomy is one hundred percent correct; I'd love to see more authors do the same.

Plate Tectonics

If you're like me, you learned the basic ideas of plate tectonics in school: giant masses of stone, some of them with water on top, floating around on the earth's mantle and making things like continents happen. But the details may have faded in your mind since then, and even if they haven't…odds are good that nobody ever talked about how these things might work, or not work, in the altered circumstances of speculative fiction.

So let's review, and then let's speculate.

I'm going to keep it fairly simple, because I'm not really qualified to get complicated. (Dammit, Jim, I'm an archaeologist, not a geologist!)

As the plates of our planetary crust move around, there are three ways they can interact: they can move apart (a divergent boundary), slam together (a convergent boundary), or slide past one another (a transform boundary). The places where these things happen are called "faults," as in the San Andreas Fault (to pick a famous example). You can roughly map the entire surface of our planet into a set of plates, though the maps you're likely to find when you search for that are simplified—there are also cratons, i.e. smaller, more stable bits inside continental plates, which is why you have faults in places like Texas, far away from any major plate boundary.

Divergent boundaries are where our planet makes new land, through the action of lava rising up and cooling into stone, pushing plates apart. Most of these are found on seafloors, though a few are on land; there's one running through East Africa and the Sinai Peninsula, whose sections are collectively known as the Great Rift Valley, which is in the (very. very. slow.) process of cracking Somalia and Ethiopia off the rest of the African Plate. The Mid-Atlantic Ridge system is, as the name suggests, largely underwater, but part of it runs through Iceland and is widening that island at a rate of a few centimeters per year.

Convergent boundaries, on the other hand, are where our planet destroys land and in the process lifts up mountains, as one plate is subducted below another and shoves that one skyward. (Remember, I'm simplifying here. Divergent boundaries form ridges along their length, too, but since most of that is deep underwater, it won't be that relevant to most stories, which tend to take place on dry land.) What kind of mountains you end up with depends on which plates are meeting: if it's two oceanic plates, you get volcanic islands in the plate that's on top. If it's a continental plate and an oceanic plate, the latter (being heavier) gets subducted under the former, so that you end up with a deep offshore trench and a volcanically active coastal mountain range—this is why we have the "Ring of Fire" around the edge of the Pacific, with ranges like the Andes. And finally, if it's two continental plates, you get the Himalayas.

Transform boundaries—like the aforementioned San Andreas fault—don't either make or destroy land, but rather slide one piece of it past another. They're a type of strike-slip fault, but this is the point at which I'm going to stop falling down a Wikipedia hole of geological research, and talk about why this matters.

To begin with, it matters because it affects what your maps should look like. Assuming you're writing about a world with plate tectonics like our own (which you might not be; more on that in a moment), it should have landforms a lot like our own. A steep, narrow range of coastal mountains like the Andes aren't likely to have extensive shallow seas with coral reefs offshore, because those types of mountains come from an oceanic plate subducting under a continental one, and that means there should be an ocean trench not too far away. A broad band of mountains like the Himalayas and their neighboring cousins aren't good candidates for extensive volcanic activity—you're more likely to find that in the aforementioned coastal range. Ever notice how West Africa looks like you could fit it between North and South America? That's because it used to be there (ish; remember that we're simplifying here). Putting a similar echo of shapes into your continental coastlines will provide a bit of subconscious verisimilitude to your map.

Does that mean you have to put together a tectonic map of your entire world? No, of course not. I did that for the Memoirs of Lady Trent (with the assistance of the guys who wrote a speculative geological history of George R.R. Martin's Westeros), but that's because I was writing about a globetrotting natural historian, and needed her natural environment to hang together sensibly. But having at least a general awareness of this means you'll know when and where to include natural disasters like earthquakes, tsunamis, and volcanic eruptions, or natural features like steam vents (fumaroles), hot springs, and dramatic rift valleys. It will help you avoid things like the infamous Square Mountains of Mordor.

Unless you *want* square mountains. This whole Patreon series is geared primarily toward speculative fiction, where there are no guarantees that the world of the story is a round ball with plate tectonics and all their associated processes. Your novel might be set on a moon covered in water ice like Europa, or a flat land like Discworld. Earthquakes might be caused by the thrashings of a bound and tortured god, rather than the sudden movement of one plate against another. Mountains could be there because a wizard decided they should.

But as with any aspect of worldbuilding, if you're going to change some basic aspect of nature from what the reader is used to, then it helps to communicate that fact, and take into account how it will affect the story. (Unless it isn't relevant to your story at all, in which case it gets the same treatment as any other background aspect you've worked out: save it for a blog post or an Easter eggs section on your website.) Characters living on a water-ice moon won't be doing very much on dry land—but they might experience ice movement very similar to plate tectonics. Characters living on a flat world won't see distant ships at sea appearing to "rise" and "sink" out of the water, because the curvature of the earth won't obscure the hull and then the masts as they get farther away. When that bound and tortured god thrashes and causes an earthquake, people will respond in ways designed to alleviate his suffering or something else to prevent further destruction.

If that last bit sounds a lot like our own world prior to the advent of things like plate tectonic theory, well, you aren't wrong. People act based on what they believe to be true, and in a fantasy world, what they believe might be physically and metaphysically correct. Or it might not be, and the reality might be something else that doesn't match our world. But whether you're talking about water-ice moons or bound gods, you want to make sure you're internally consistent.

Rivers

Moving on from the planetary scale, let's talk about rivers: how they work, how they're used, and how *not* to do them.

Starting with that last point. And as my illustrative example, I'm going to use something that is both near and dear to my heart and hydrologically nonsensical: the empire of Rokugan from the game *Legend of the Five Rings*.

The map has varied slightly from edition to edition, not just in style but in geography; you can see several versions if you search onlinw. The inconsistencies are traditionally explained away by in-world reasons: pre-modern cartography is not a precise art, and besides which, the various powers that be have a vested interest in making sure they're the only ones with accurate maps. In general I'm fine with this...but it only goes so far, and the behavior of the rivers is one of the places where it breaks down for me.

Take a good look at Rokugan. And then look at, say, the Mississippi River basin.

The latter example has a generally fan-like shape: rivers go from areas of higher elevation (the Rocky Mountains, the Appalachian Mountains) toward lower elevations, for the simple reason that water flows downhill. As they do so, they join together to make bigger rivers, until ultimately all of them feed in to the Mississippi—which is why we call this a drainage basin.

It's a region that all drains to the same point, which is the mouth of the Mississippi River, emptying out into the ocean. (You can also have an endorheic basin, with no outlet to the sea: it all converges to a lake or swamp and evaporates from there.) Rivers in Rokugan do not join together. They separate. In the most recent edition, in the northwest there's a lake whose outflow descends from the mountains: okay. But then...does that river split? Or is the western branch actually another river joining up with the eastern branch (which apparently flows through a small mountain range)? Only for that to be true, you have to assume that the major river running from northwest to southeast is the one that splits—just like the one due south of the mountains, down near the coast—or the lake in the eastern edge of the mountains, that somehow both flows north through the mountains and south to the sea—and the tiny little river along the coast that inexplicably has enough flow to form both a substantial bay and split off to form the biggest delta in the Empire—and let's not even talk about what's happening in the big patch of mountains at the very bottom of the map. It's the setting's equivalent of Mordor; we'll chalk the incoherence there up to evil magic and move on.

Now, as some fans of L5R have pointed out, there are a very very few instances in nature where rivers naturally diverge—not parting to go around an island before rejoining, but truly splitting. (I think the frequency with which it happens here argues for "mistake" rather than "deliberate choice" but I could be wrong.) Furthermore, because Rokugan is a fantasy setting, you can always say "but magic" and call it a day.

However, if you do that? You have to *do* that. Make it clear to the reader that this is a setting where the normal laws of nature do not apply: rivers diverge instead of converging (and don't become smaller as a result), water flows uphill in its determination to cross a mountain range, etc.

You also have to realize that if you do that, you're screwing with the logic that underpins how human societies relate to waterways. Cities were often founded along rivers not only because they provide a ready source of water, but because they provide a natural highway for travel and transporting goods.

Putting things on a barge and floating them downstream is often a good deal easier than hauling them across dry land. Going upstream is harder, but still possible, and possibly even still easier: barring obstacles like rapids, shallows, or waterfalls (which you can sometimes portage around), you're looking at what is literally the path of least resistance, because that's the route water likes to take.

But this peters out as you go farther into the fringes of the drainage basin, because the rivers there get smaller and smaller. Large barges can't make it past a certain point; you have to switch to smaller ones, or little craft like rowboats and canoes, with a shallow enough draft to navigate the shallower waters. So the effectiveness of trade along the waterways depends on where you are in them. And, of course, you may find yourself with a geography where it's actually easier to haul your goods along the land—even if there's something like a mountain range in the way—to get at a more useful bit of river, rather than taking the long way around with the local water.

Confluences are great places to stick your city because then you control the traffic on multiple rivers. So are fords—places where the river is shallow enough to be crossed without a bridge—or, when you get the technology for it, the bridges themselves. Being at the mouth of a river is excellent, because then you get access to sea trade *and* everything heading into or out of the river system. But if there's a big estuary or a delta, you're frequently better off being far enough upriver to avoid the brackish water or divergent channels (deltas being one of the few places where a river diverging makes sense, because it's essentially a giant mudflat).

All of this means that paying attention to how your rivers work isn't just a matter of geography; it's also a question of cultural worldbuilding. In high school I drew a map for my Nine Lands stories that originally featured a river which flowed all the way from one coast to another, and it took me an embarrassingly long time to notice what I'd done. I would have had a hard time saying anything plausible about trade on that river, because I wouldn't even have been able to tell you which direction it flowed in. Waterways also affect warfare, by influencing everything from borders to troop movements to what counts as a strategic target.

If you want those things to feel real, it helps for the land they take place on to feel real, too.

Mountains

Mountains are inextricably involved with the tectonic processes that shape our whole planet. But they're also a geographical feature writers often stick into their invented worlds, so let's take a look at them in more detail—this time not with an eye toward how they're made, but rather toward how human beings relate to them.

(Disclaimer: I grew up in Texas. In the *Great Plains* part of Texas. The highest elevation in my immediate vicinity was probably a highway overpass. My personal, direct experience of mountains is...limited.)

To begin with, you should ask yourself what type of mountains you're looking at. Are these old and weathered mountains like the Appalachians, not too high and not too rugged? Or are they newer creations like the Rockies or the Himalayas? Do they rise high enough to have permanent snow caps, or does it all melt off in the warmer seasons? How much water is found there? Are they volcanically active?

As a corollary to this, you should be aware of the physical effects mountains have on the weather. When wind blows toward a mountain range and is pushed upward by the rising elevation, it cools and can form clouds—which, when close to the ground, will look like fog—which may then bring rain. The windward side of a mountain will typically get more rainfall than the leeward side; the latter falls in a "rain shadow," and as the air descends that side and warms up, it generates a dry, gusty wind that in the western United States is sometimes called a chinook.

(Fun fact: lenticular or "lens-shaped" clouds can form over mountain peaks, and may be one of the causes of purported UFO sightings. Actually, there are a whole bunch of interesting things that can happen to clouds around mountains; if you want to make your description of such a region feel vivid, take a few minutes to look them up.)

Moving to the social side...unsurprisingly, mountains tend to take on a lot of importance in human perception. After all, they're *big*. And less user-friendly than plains. It's no wonder that they crop up again and again in world mythology; many gods are associated with the sky, and since mountains get closer to the heavens than any other land form, of course that's where they'll dwell, whether it's Mount Olympus or Mount Meru or the Jade Mountain. We'll talk in a later volume about the concept of the Axis Mundi, the "cosmic center," but for now, let's just say that mountains are one of the most common ways to conceive of such a thing.

They also tend to be comparatively wild, because they're difficult to travel through or cultivate. Terracing is possible, but very labor-intensive, and it doesn't work everywhere: if there's heavy late-season snowfall, or insufficient water, or very rocky soil, or a slope too steep to cut usable tiers from it, then it isn't arable (i.e. suitable for cultivation). Any wealth you extract from such terrain is likely to be in the form of minerals—stone or metals—or renewable resources like lumber or fur or the produce of hardy creatures like goats. Or you just let nature keep the place, and live in the lowlands, with one eye on the wild heights from which wolves and stranger things may come.

Mountains create isolation. Rivers descending from them are often too steep and torrential to be navigable; roads are difficult to cut and often get obliterated by washouts and rockfalls. Goods may have to be transported on foot, or on the backs of pack animals hardy enough to manage the terrain—which horses often aren't, being natives of steppe grasslands. (You're better off with donkeys, mules, or llamas.) Any given mountain valley might be cut off from the rest of the world for months out of the year, if there's heavy snow at higher elevations, and even in the summer it's not very accessible. This has effects on the culture of such places, which will often feature very individualized customs not found elsewhere. The stereotype of an impenetrable mountain dialect and a clannish wariness toward outsiders is founded in reality.

Thanks to the difficulties posed by traveling across mountains, a range makes for a very natural boundary between places, especially neighboring countries. In pre-modern times, that boundary is liable to be very fuzzy; the western side of the mountains belongs to Country A and the eastern to Country B, but you won't find a nice clear line drawn along the ground in the middle. This is part of why you get border skirmishes, with one government getting annoyed that settlers or prospectors from a neighboring land are encroaching on their territory.

The one place where a boundary is likely to be very clear is in a pass, because that's a strategically important location. Passes, being the points at which you can cross a range with relative ease, are the route most trade and travel will take; they're also natural choke-points. Controlling one means you control who goes through, allowing you to tax or document or turn back anybody you like. It isn't uncommon to have a fortress to guard the place, maybe not in the pass itself—because there probably isn't a lot of extra room up there, not to mention that first constructing and then supplying the place will be a massive pain in the neck—but somewhere nearby, monitoring the road and the surrounding terrain.

Because of course people are going to try to slip by. Smugglers are as much of a thing in the mountains as they are at sea, taking little back paths too small or dangerous for the big caravans. Sometimes military forces can do the same thing, overrunning that fort in a surprise attack and then letting the main army come swarming through unopposed. One of the theory posts at the end of this volume will discuss "liminality," the concept possessed by things that stand on or across boundaries; here it is in very practical action. Borders are dangerous places, and mountains are a border: between countries, between land and sky, between the world of civilization and that of nature or the gods.

Deserts

There are a lot of different types of terrain I could theoretically discuss, but since I don't want to spend too long on that general topic at one time, let's close out this section with deserts, and come back to the natural landscape again in a future volume.

Starting again with the foundations: where do you find deserts? It depends on how they're formed. The "horse latitudes" between 30 and 35 degrees north or south are responsible for many of the deserts you think of when you hear the word—the Sahara, the Kalahari, the deserts of the Middle East and the southwestern United States, and so forth—because the behavior of the prevailing winds there creates frequently dry and sunny weather. I mentioned rain shadows before; a severe one can create a desert or at least a semi-arid region on the leeward side of a mountain range. The interior of a large continent is a good candidate for aridity, simply because the region is far from any major sources of water, such that air masses have long since lost the moisture they picked up previously. But coastal deserts like the Atacama are possible, too; these are found where the ocean waters are cold and therefore contribute less moisture, and are often helped along by mountains.

You also find deserts in books. But oh man, they are so often written by people who have apparently never been in one.

Toss in some vague descriptions of scorching heat and sand dunes, add a camel or two for color, nod toward the idea that water is precious, and you're done, right?

Not so much.

First of all, let's bear in mind that deserts are not necessarily hot. What are the two largest deserts on Earth? Antarctica, followed by the Arctic. A desert is defined scientifically by its scant precipitation, and less formally by its dearth of vegetation; by either metric, both of those qualify in spades. In fact, it's only logical that our polar regions should be arid, because air that cold is incapable of carrying very much moisture. If you read a story about a polar explorer getting buried in a massive snowfall, that writer probably hasn't done their research—though it's quite possible for existing snow to blow around in a ground blizzard, and to pile up in dunes much like the sand-based ones we associate with the word "desert."

Sand isn't a required feature of hot deserts, though. In fact, though sand and extensive seas of dunes (known as ergs) are fairly common in Central Asian deserts, making up a little less than half of their total area, that's almost non-existent in North American deserts, which are instead quite rocky. If there are large stony outcroppings, erosion from either wind or water can leave you with fascinating formations: Monument Valley in the United States is an very well-known example, having been featured in countless film Westerns.

It also isn't necessarily the case that a desert is barren. In many cases the limited precipitation falls in a clear seasonal pattern, rather than being evenly distributed across the year, and when the rains arrive, the desert springs to life. It doesn't transform into Ireland, of course, but plants that were dry and scrubby put out their fresh new growth, and places you would have sworn had no plant life at all may suddenly be carpeted in flowers. Residents of such areas take advantage of this, gathering and preserving food for the dry season, fattening up their herds on the water-rich pasturage, and so on. And even when the rains don't fall, life persists in all kinds of ingenious ways.

The part about water being scarce is true, though. If there isn't some major river like the Nile nearby, your characters are going to need to be careful, making sure they know how to find water and rationing what they have until they reach the next supply. Depending on the politics of the area, water sources may be controlled by different groups, and it's possible to exhaust a tiny spring and have to wait a long time for it to refill. Bathing in a tub full of water is probably Right Out; Islamic law even makes an allowance for "washing" yourself with sand before praying, if water is too scarce to spend on ritual ablutions.

One of the keys to survival is knowing how to get your hydration from organisms that are better at it than you are. Camels can extract moisture from plants inedible to humans, so if you travel with a string of milch camels, you can graze them and then drink their milk. Cactus fruit can also help you out—but beware the cartoons that lead you to believe there are reservoirs of potable water inside the plant itself. The liquid you get from most species is loaded with toxins that will actually make things worse for you.

It also helps to know when to travel. Even in a hot desert, the night is often frigid, because the dry air doesn't retain heat very well. Experienced travelers will often move from dawn until noon or thereabouts, rest for a few hours, then start up again in the evening and go until late at night before resting again. This lets them shelter from both the hottest and coldest parts of the cycle, taking advantage of the milder times to cover ground.

Sandstorms are a real danger if you're in an area of extensive sand, and in general wind erosion is going to be a constant factor, because of all the particulate matter blown around. But water can also be a threat: if the ground is dry, and then seasonal precipitation shows up in the form of a thunderstorm, a large percentage of that is going to become runoff rather than soaking into the ground, creating flash floods. When one of those slams through a gully or slot canyon, it can kill you in no time flat. (This can strike even if you aren't being rained on directly. If the storm is happening upstream of you, the runoff will hit you from above, and often without warning.)

And don't forget about sunburn! Not only do you have to worry about the sun beating down on you from above, but also the light reflecting up from the sand or stone. In a hot desert it may be tempting to strip down to minimal clothing, but unless you're blessed with abundant melanin, you're going to wind up regretting that. (We aren't only talking about reddened skin, either. A severe sunburn can produce blisters, fainting, and worse.) Loose robes have the advantage of full coverage while also allowing for more air circulation inside than tight-fitting shirts and trousers. You may also need to protect your eyes from the constant brightness or wind-borne dust; eye problems are *very* common in desert-dwelling populations.

So in the end, deserts make for good storytelling, because they pose such dramatic challenges to the traveler, and constrain the societies living there in ways that are deeply unfamiliar to your average temperate-zone-dwelling reader. But as with so many things, do your research: once you know what kind of desert you're talking about, read up on the cultures that have adapted to such a place, whether that's the Bedouin or the Hopi or the Uyghurs. Everything from their foodways to their governmental structure will teach you things about how people survive in that terrain, and help you set your tale in something more specific than a basic cartoon desert.

Natural Disasters

When "natural disasters" wandered through my head as a possible thing to write about, I found myself thinking, *Is that really a worldbuilding topic? Aren't natural disasters more of a plot element?*

That type of thinking is exactly why I want to talk about natural disasters as an aspect of worldbuilding.

Let me illustrate with two real-life stories. I have a friend I often visit in New York City whose apartment has very deep molding around the doors and windows. She has decorated these with small spheres of different kinds of stone, on little stands—it's very pretty. But the first time I visited her after moving to California, I looked up at those and twitched. *Man, those are all going to fall on somebody's head in the first earthquake.*

Also, earlier this year a friend of mine moved from California (where he's lived his whole life) to Texas (where I grew up). When he asked what he should know about his new home, one of the first things I did was educate him in tornado safety: he'd never even thought about it before.

In stories, natural disasters usually *are* plot. Blizzards happen when you need to trap your characters in their current location. Earthquakes happen when dead gods rise. Volcanoes exist for the purpose of melting magical rings. You almost never hear about such things outside of those moments—even though many of us live in places where they're an ever-present concern, albeit a background one. Flooding. Hurricanes. Ashfall from the nearby volcano. Mudslides. Wildfires. Tsunami. There are a *lot* of ways the world around you can go wrong. Sometimes it may be intentional—the evil sorcerer controlling the elements, the alien empire using weapons beyond our ken, the angry god punishing impiety—but even in the absence of such forces, these things will just happen, as the inevitable consequence of natural forces at work.

Why bring up such things when they aren't plot-relevant? For the same reason you provide any other sort of descriptive detail: because it gives your setting depth, makes it feel more three-dimensional and real. Your readers from California or Japan will feel a little frisson of recognition when a small tremor shakes the ground beneath your protagonist, making her pause briefly and look for the nearest sheltered spot before continuing on with her business. That volcanic ashfall can be a source of tension; your characters are used to it and sweeping away the day's ash is part of their routine, but the reader wonders if it's foreshadowing, a harbinger of greater trouble to come. Maybe people keep small rowboats at their houses because the river floods every spring and trying to walk or ride to the neighbor's house will be impossible for a month or so. The flood doesn't have to be disastrous for you to include that little moment of color, paddling around on one's errands instead of going by dry land. (In the canal region of Kerala in India, going places via boat is quite common.)

These hazards shape our architecture. Many places in the "Tornado Alley" corridor of the Midwestern U.S. have basements or other underground refuges where you can go when the sky threatens to unload a twister. Roofs in wintry regions are steep rather than flat, the better to shed their burden of snow. People in flood-prone regions may put their houses on stilts or small rises, clear of the expected water level; people in earthquake-prone coastal regions may build their houses on higher elevations away from the shoreline, to avoid the destruction of a tsunami. (There are markers showing the point below which you should not build in northern Japan, which were ignored by more recent generations. The Sendai earthquake in 2011 reminded everyone why those markers were there.) Even on a smaller scale, kitchens are sometimes built as free-standing structures not only to keep the smells of food preparation away from the living quarters, but also so they won't take out the whole house when the inevitable fire happens.

As my stories above illustrate, such hazards also shape our behavior. A New Englander will put a beautiful glass vase on a little pedestal above a tile floor; a Californian may cringe at the sight of it, envisioning shards flying everywhere at the first tremor. A resident of Tornado Alley will take note of certain weather conditions (the green sky is proverbial, but not always accurate) and reflexively calculate the best place to shelter, should it be necessary. A Norwegian won't put important objects outside in the winter, where they might get glued down with ice or buried under three feet of snow. Failing to pay attention to this sort of thing risks kicking the knowledgeable reader straight out of the story: I happily bought into the alien powers and kryptonite of the TV show *Smallville*, but when they showed me a Midwestern girl trying to drive away from a tornado rather than lying down in a ditch, my suspension of disbelief died on the spot.

And since we're talking about speculative fiction: you can always invent new hazards. In C.S. Friedman's Coldfire Trilogy, many of the biggest threats on her alien planet come from "fae," which are not sentient creatures so much as a kind of substance that responds to human thought. It comes in several different types, and the most dangerously volatile type, dark fae, cannot survive the light. Which means you're fine...until "true night" falls. When the Core (the massed stars of the Milky Way, on whose extreme fringes this star system is found) and the sun and the moons have all set? Then things get very bad. That kind of thing veers back toward plot-central disaster, but it's also very clearly an element of the worldbuilding, because of the precautions people take when true night is about to occur. It adds a new wrinkle to the setting that has repercussions for the way all the characters live.

The natural world may be a background element rather than a driver of your plot, but that doesn't mean it isn't there—or that it can't pose hazards to your characters. How many of you reading this live in a place where some potential disaster or another is a concern? Now ask yourself how often you've seen that in a story...and whether you can put it into one of your own.

How Many Seasons?

"I miss seasons."

I hear this sometimes from people who move to the San Francisco Bay Area from the East Coast or the Midwest of the United States. Truth be told, it gets up my nose a little bit more every time I hear it—to the point where sometimes instead of smiling and nodding, I tell the truth:

"We *have* seasons. They're just not the ones you're used to."

Spring, summer, autumn, winter. Summer (roughly June-August) is hot and may have thunderstorms. Winter (roughly December-February) is cold and should have snow. Spring is the March-May transition where all the dormant plants start growing again and everything is bright green and the flowers bloom. Autumn is the September-November transition where the leaves turn pretty colors and fall off and there might be frost at night, which I'm told is delightful if you like that sort of thing. It is acceptable to live in a place where summer is more like April-October (Texas, where I grew up) or winter shows up in November and stays until March. But you are still assumed to have the standard-issue four seasons out of the year, with some of them compressed to make room for the big one.

Because you're assumed to live in a temperate continental environment.

Where I live now, though, our climate more closely resembles the Mediterranean than Massachusetts. Like the tropics, we basically have two seasons: wet and dry. The wet season can happen anywhere in the October-March window, depending on the year and what the effects of climate change are like this time around, but it's a mistake to assume the calendrical overlap means that it's winter by another name: 'round here, this is when things *grow*. Crops thrive in the mid-year months because of irrigation, but the natural vegetation is more inclined to go dormant, the hillsides turning gold as the grass dies. Come the rains, all that will be green again—in December or January. Contrary to what you learned in grade school, Persephone is in Hades during the *summer*; she's reunited with Demeter in the autumn, when the new crops are planted.

When people talk about how cold the summers are in San Francisco, that's partly because they're assuming our warm weather should show up according to the temperate zone schedule. But atmospheric conditions mean that we may have what the southern California coast calls "June gloom"—a period of overcast weather and cool temperatures that occurs in part because of our characteristic marine layer (source of all that fog). Summer—by which I mean warm weather—often doesn't arrive until more like August, September, even October…the first year I lived in the Bay Area, our hottest days came the week before Thanksgiving. (Not kidding.) As an absolute measure the average high temperatures for this area aren't going to compete with places like Texas, but the curve is different, too.

This means that if you look around the world, you find that the four-season model doesn't always apply. Some places have the two seasons I just described, the wet and the dry. Others have six: prevernal (early spring), vernal (spring), estival (high summer), serotinal (late summer), autumnal (autumn), and hibernal (winter). In some regions of India, it's spring, summer, monsoon, autumn, late autumn/early winter, and late winter/prevernal (those of course being English glosses of the local terms). Indigenous Australians have multiple different approaches, varying based on which part of Australia you're talking about—which is only logical, when you think about the ecological diversity across that continent. The core concept behind a "season" is that it maps to the shifts in vegetation, animal behavior, temperature, and precipitation that occur during the course of a year; ergo, your natural (as opposed to calendrical) seasons will depend on where you live

So when you think about the seasons of your setting, two different angles can come into play. First, what is the environment like where the story takes place? And second, where did they get their calendar from? The words "spring" or "autumn" might never pass the lips of your tropics-dwelling characters, who speak only of the wet season and the dry season. But people in a temperate environment might dutifully talk about the upcoming monsoon season, even though there will be no monsoon, because they got their calendar from an imperial power that originated in a place that *does* have one. Do your spacefaring colonists keep the calendar of their home despite living on a planet where the year is 592 days long, or do they adapt to the new schedule? You might be writing about a world like George R.R. Martin's Westeros, where the seasons appear to have bugger-all to do with the yearly round. Heck, you could make up your own seasons, based either on an alien ecology (natural seasons) or the cultural division of time (calendrical seasons). Want to have three divisions to the year, or seven? Go for it.

And then, for the love of little raindrops: remember the seasons are *there*. This applies to any kind of fiction, even the ones that aren't speculative at all. What time of year is your story taking place? What does that mean for the weather? Does enough time pass during the story that the seasons are going to change? What does that mean for your characters? I sometimes wonder if TV deserves some blame for stories where everyone seems to live in a season-free bubble. The logistics of filming (your location, protecting your equipment, maintaining continuity, the potential mismatch between time inside and outside of the story) mean that precipitation of either the liquid or frozen kind only shows up on special occasions (it's a Christmas episode; time for snow!), and the characters seem to wear the same clothes all year round. Unless you happen to glimpse a leafless tree in the background, it's difficult-to-impossible to guess what time of year it is from natural cues.

I'm nearly three seasons into *Haven*, a show set in Maine, and I don't think I've seen a single snowflake pass the camera's lens. Even if your characters live in a city, the planet still turns and the world still changes around them. They build up the fire or turn down the thermostat or grab their waterproof outer layers, like you and I do every day. As with so many of these details, remembering that makes the world of the story feel more physically persuasive.

Measuring Time

In talking about seasons, I mentioned George R.R. Martin's *A Song of Ice and Fire*, where the variation in weather seems to have nothing whatsoever to do with the yearly round. What *is* the yearly round? How do we define a "year"?

That's a much more complicated question than you might think. A year is the length of time it takes the planet to go one orbit around the sun…but measuring that requires a fair bit of skill. When you hear about places like Newgrange, where the building is constructed such that the light of the rising sun on the winter solstice will shine into the inner chamber, that's the kind of method ancient people used to measure a year. It comes out to 365 days, more or less—but it's the "more or less" part that will trip you up. Really it's closer to 365.25 days, which is why in the Gregorian calendar we get leap days every four years (unless the year is divisible by 100 (unless the year is divisible by 400)). We have to play catch-up with the planet.

If you measure the year by the lunar cycle instead, as cultures ranging from the Hebrews and Muslims to Chinese, Nepali, and Mongolians have done, you have a year that's about 354 days long, and over time the dates of that calendar will go walkabout through the seasons—Christmas would be a winter, spring, summer, or autumn holiday depending on the year in question. If you hybridize the two into a lunisolar calendar, you add leap months every so often to prevent the schedule from wandering too far afield. You can have a vague year, a heliacal year, a draconic year (man, I missed my chance to use that in the Memoirs of Lady Trent)—there are all kinds of ways to measure time and then call it a year.

Of course—since we're talking about speculative fiction—you don't *have* to deal with this 365.2425 day nonsense. You could make a year in your setting a nice round 365 days, or even 360, which is cleanly divisible by all kinds of numbers. Or any other figure you like. You could have the cycle of the moon(s) match perfectly to the solar year, instead of being about 11 days off. Too tidy of an answer would probably seem out of place in planetary science fiction, but in secondary-world fantasy there's no reason it can't be as tidy as you like—or as messy. Don't believe there's plot potential in the question of how to measure a year? The switch from the Julian to the Gregorian calendar was *hugely* political in Renaissance Europe, to the point where Protestant Britain resisted adopting that Catholic-driven change for nearly two hundred years after everyone else got on board. The hexarchate in Yoon Ha Lee's *Ninefox Gambit* maintains its control through manipulation of the calendar in its territory, and builds technologies based on the metaphysical effects of that calendar.

On a finer-grained level: how does the society measure months? Are they directly mapped to the lunar cycle, an approximation of it, completely unrelated? *Are* there months? How about weeks—do those exist? Most readers these days are going to be accustomed to a seven-day cycle, but the Roman week was eight days long, based around the timing of markets. There's evidence for every length of week ranging from ten all the way down to one—I'm really not clear on how the Pawukon is supposed to work.

Or you can step out to the macro level and consider eras. We're used to the Common Era/Anno Domini approach that counts years up from a starting date, but it's not uncommon to instead count the years of the ruler's reign; this is how the traditional Japanese calendar handles it (2017 is Heisei 29), and historical English documents often gloss the time with the same information.

NEW WORLDS, YEAR ONE

There's also the concept of an "indiction," which is a fifteen-year cycle used in medieval Europe—or later on, it meant any individual year within that cycle, as the terminology changed from "year one of the indiction" to "first indiction." This had its origins in third-century Roman Egyptian taxation schedules, but morphed a great deal through the centuries. I sometimes wonder if it influenced the *Dragon Age* multimedia franchise, where every hundred-year epoch is given a name based on omens that appear at the end of the previous era—so when they talk about the Dragon Age, they literally mean the year is 9:30 Dragon, the thirtieth year of the ninth age, which is called Dragon.

Names are part of the reason why thinking about these things can be worth your time and effort. Even if you don't want to delve into the philosophical implications of how your fictional society divides time, the names of days, weeks, months, years, eras, etc. add detail to their culture. Where do those names come from: gods, seasonal markers, ordinary numbers, historical rulers, flowers of great symbolic significance, holy virtues? Or a mix, like our own days of the week and months of the year? (As the name implies, December was originally the tenth month instead of the twelfth.) You can interweave this with the rest of your worldbuilding, so that a) you don't have to make up the names out of nowhere and b) your reader gets a subconscious impression of what that society considers important.

And while you're at it, take a moment to consider when things start. Want to know why many countries have taxes due in April? Because the year used to start in the spring, rather than an arbitrary date in winter. Oddly, though a number of calendars had the year begin somewhere in the vicinity of the vernal or autumnal equinox, solstices don't seem to be popular for that purpose; our January 1st date is about as close as you get. The rest seem to be fairly disconnected from astronomical markers.

Days, however, tend to be very closely linked to the sun. In the absence of mechanical clocks (which are expensive and difficult to make), many cultures have measured the day as

35

starting either with dawn or with sunset, rather than in the middle of the night. This still crops up folklorically and in fictional magic systems, where supernatural effects often start or expire at those times. But if you go the sunset route, be careful with your dialogue: the reader is going to instinctively assume that "yesterday," when said in the evening, means more than twenty hours before, not four. (The same is true of sunrise, but characters are rarely doing much before dawn.)

Where Does the Food Come From?

At science fiction and fantasy conventions, there are often panels about food—or rather, who writes about it vividly. The reason we have these panels is that many authors *don't* really write about food: where we get it from, what we eat, and what kinds of practices we build up around those things.

On the science fictional end, you sometimes see the assumption that the only real purpose of food is to provide us with nutrients and calories, and therefore in the future we will all be glad to get those from pellets; this completely ignores the social and sensory aspects of meals. On the fantasy end, Diana Wynne Jones' *Tough Guide to Fantasyland* mocked the ubiquity of stew—a trope that showed up in a lot of novels for a while because the authors basically didn't think about the foodways of their worlds at all and simply plugged in what they thought of as a Generic Meal.

Let's start with the basics: what archaeologists and anthropologists refer to as subsistence strategies.

This isn't a very sexy term, or even a very sexy topic—but most if not all of us are used to thinking of food as something you get from a grocery store. We're so disconnected from the actual process of feeding a community that it's invisible to us, and as a result, we don't think about how it works for the communities we write about.

Subsistence strategies fall into two broad categories: foraging and production. Foraging is the exploitation of wild resources, while production brings that under human control, making rather than acquiring food for people to eat. The shift between the two is an earth-shaking one, profoundly transforming society.

Let's talk about foraging first. This is also called "hunting and gathering," though sometimes anthropologists will use other terms as well, like "collecting" for the process of harvesting stationary animal resources like eggs or clams, or "scavenging" for taking other creatures' kills. Most people (including a sad number of past anthropologists) used to put the emphasis in that phrase on *hunting*, assuming that it provided the bulk of people's food, with gathering basically providing a side salad.

But the truth is that studies of modern hunter-gatherers—admittedly in fairly marginal lands—show they succeed at taking prey maybe one hunt in four. Quite a lot of the caloric intake of a foraging society comes from a huge variety of wild plant sources, and when animal protein shows up, it's often from collectible sources or small trappable prey like birds, rabbits, or fish, rather than big impressive game like deer and bear. Hunting larger animals is quite frankly dangerous, as we see from broken bones in the archaeological record. But it's also more glamorous, and mostly associated with men rather than women, so for a long time there was a bias toward paying attention to that and downplaying the importance of gathering.

Foraging imposes some limitations on a society. The usual rule of thumb is that a hunter-gatherer group will be a band of roughly twenty-five to fifty people, because that's how many you can feed with the resources within a reasonable walking distance—get beyond that and you start burning more calories than it's worth. This varies depending on the environment, though. Likewise, foraging societies are almost always mobile, moving on when they've exhausted the resources in one area, or migrating to exploit seasonal abundance in a certain place...but there are environments, like the Pacific Northwest, where it's possible to support a large sedentary population just off wild food sources.

Sedentarism usually accompanies agriculture because agriculture creates more human-edible calories per acre of land than a natural environment does. The intermediate step here is usually called horticulture, i.e. the small-scale growing of food, and may have started with humans trying to encourage wild stands of grains. The animal side of things is pastoralism, i.e. the herding of livestock like horses, camels, cows, pigs, sheep, goats, chickens, and more.

Once you ramp up from horticulture to agriculture, you get a whole host of changes: permanent settlements (because you have to stay and look after your fields), population explosion (because you can feed so many more people and don't have to worry about small children making long journeys), increased specialization (because food abundance means more people can skip engaging in food production and spend their time on other tasks), malnutrition and famine (because people are relying on a much smaller range of food sources and are more vulnerable to crop failures), social stratification (because of increased wealth and increased need for organization to manage everything), more widespread infectious disease (because dense sedentary populations offer more opportunity for its spread), a spike in interpersonal violence—in fact, Jared Diamond wrote an article called "The Worst Mistake in the History of the Human Race," and while the title is deliberately provocative, the article itself is an antidote to the assumption that early agriculture was an unmitigated blessing. Without it we wouldn't have anything like the society we live in today—but it came with a lot of costs that aren't obvious in these days of mechanized production.

The vast majority of our novels and short stories take place in societies that rely more on food production than foraging. (Even in a science fictional future where meat is being grown in vats, that's still production.) But foraging shows up here and there: in epic fantasies when the characters are bushwhacking across the wilderness, in post-apocalyptic stories where agriculture and shipping have broken down, in survival stories where the characters are stranded in the middle of nowhere. Unfortunately, many of the writers who include that type of thing often seem to have very little understanding of how it works.

And even when production is assumed, authors often fail to think about any of the pragmatic requirements. You get cities in the middle of nowhere, with no sign of the fields that ought to support them or the infrastructure that would bring food to them; you get abundant consumption of meat without the pastures necessary to feed the livestock. Take a moment to look at something you're writing or reading and ask yourself: do you know where their food comes from and how? If you don't know, does a sensible answer fit easily into the picture you see? Or is this like Lothlórien, with no sign of the fields or the farmers who produce the ingredients for *lembas*, let alone anything else the elves eat?

It doesn't have to play a role in every story. But it doesn't hurt to think about it, either.

Local and Imported Food

Paying a little bit of attention to the food your characters eat can go a long way toward making your invented world feel real and lived-in and coherent.

Let's start with something basic: what's the staple grain? Taking a moment to specify whether it's wheat, millet, oats, barley, rye, rice, maize, amaranth, or quinoa pops the world briefly into three dimensions. What fruits are available? If it's a temperate climate, things like pineapples, mangos, and guava will be out of place. If your characters are tramping around a tropical jungle, having them stumble across blueberries or pears would be implausible. If the people keep livestock, what kind? Chickens have proved capable of thriving damn near anywhere; so have pigs, though they're more likely than chickens to be the subjects of dietary taboos. Other creatures need a lot more pasturage or are pickier about their environmental tolerances. For cows to work, there needs to be quite a lot of grass available; in dry climates you'll do better with goats or camels.

There are a great many edible plants and animals that we tend not to think about today because they aren't amenable to modern industrial production, or have been replaced by alternatives that are tastier or more nutritious or easier to prepare. This seems to be especially true of fowl: these days I only occasionally see duck in a non-Chinese restaurant, but Europeans used to regularly consume duck, pigeon, swan, grouse, and more. Ditto for other small animals, like rabbits—

or in other parts of the world, dogs and cats, and horses and camels on the larger end of things.

And even if it's something we still eat today, don't assume that its cultural role has always been the same. For centuries oysters were a cheap London street food, before the pollution of the Thames drove stocks into a decline. Lobster was despised as fit only for the poor; in the U.S. they regularly served it to prison inmates, which is unthinkable today. (Though there is apparently no historical evidence for the common assertion that servants' contracts specified they would not have to eat lobster more than twice a week.)

What about the form the food takes? Some things are essentially universal, like soups and stews, or the art of wrapping something edible in something else edible—whether you call the latter a taco, a spring roll, or a dürüm. People around the world have always experimented with fermenting anything they can, from rice to grapes to milk to sharks. Other types of food are not necessarily as widespread as you might think, like leavened bread. We sometimes talk about the role of estrangement in speculative fiction—causing the reader to see a familiar thing in a new light—and this is an easy place to do that; have a traveling character recoil when offered lumps of curdled milk, aka cheese. (I had fun with this one in the Memoirs of Lady Trent, where the protagonist is raised in a Judaism-based religion and is horrified to discover that while ill in a foreign country, she was fed a broth with "pig meat" in it. If you don't consider pigs to be food, you aren't going to have the word "pork" in your vocabulary.)

That leads us to the question of imported foods, which can also add a lot of color to the story. What kinds of things do your societies have the capability of importing, and what is considered worth the effort?

It's easy to forget nowadays, with many grocery stores stocking produce from all around the world, but in the days before refrigeration and fast long-distance travel, the food available in any given place would often be pretty limited, and imports could be ludicrously expensive. Historically spices have been a tremendously desirable cargo because their value-to-volume ratio is high, and they keep well enough to survive a lengthy journey—and when I say "spices," I don't just mean the ones that are still expensive today (like saffron), but things we now consider to be utterly ordinary, like salt and black pepper. I'm told that the very first edition of Julia Child's cookbook introduced the average American reader to an exotic herb called "thyme" and explained how to get your local grocer to order it in—thyme! One of the least unusual things in my spice cabinet! But fifty years ago, things were different.

Other foodstuffs don't travel so well. In the trailer for the movie *Victoria and Abdul*, Queen Victoria's manservant Abdul Karim tells her about the fruit of his native India, which leads her to demand that a mango be shipped to England. Even with Victorian innovations to help, when it arrives it is...an ex-mango. Some things could be packed in ice, but prior to refrigeration technology ice was only available in some seasons and some locales, which were often not the places producing exotic fruits.

The better solution was to try and transplant the exotics directly. If you wanted oranges in Renaissance England, you could import them from Spain, or you could build a greenhouse and grow your own. They might not be as good, thanks to the different climate, but they'd be a lot cheaper. In the nineteenth century Britain went to great lengths to smuggle tea plants out of China so they could break the monopoly on that trade by growing their own supply in India. Animals pose more of a problem; importing enough living specimens to start a breeding population is difficult, especially since some animals travel even less well alive than they do dead and unrefrigerated.

I should also bring up the Columbian Exchange, i.e. the massive transfer of species between the Old World and the New. It's no accident that the Thanksgiving menu often features things like turkey, potato, pumpkin, corn, cranberry, and sweet potato, all of which are indigenous to the New World. Some readers will get kicked out of the story if you cross your culinary streams, e.g. by having tomatoes in the very European-feeling setting of *The Lord of the Rings*. (Italian food without tomatoes! It seems unthinkable...but that really only became a thing in the nineteenth century.) Me, I don't mind it; as long as the climate is appropriate, there's no reason you couldn't find plants and animals from different parts of the real world occupying the same region of an invented world, even before they have the trade necessary to introduce lots of invasive species.

But if you're worried about that kind of thing, do a bit of research into the food that was eaten in a given place and time comparable to the society you're writing about. Then your characters can eat fufu or nattō instead of generic stew or roast beast, and maybe you'll be mentioned on a panel someday about authors who write vividly about food.

Kitchens

If you're anything like me, you take kitchens for granted.

I mean, every house has one, right? There are some apartments that don't, but even there, the assumption tends to be that it'll have a kitchen—however tiny it may be—and the ones without are the exception. But that assumption rests on the modern conveniences of indoor plumbing, refrigeration, ovens and stoves, supplemented by microwaves and hot plates and toasters and everything else we use to preserve and cook our food and clean up the mess afterward.

Take those away, and it's a very different picture. A much more hazardous one, too.

Let's start with food prep. Two hundred years ago, if you wanted to roast a chicken for dinner, you didn't go buy a refrigerated carcass from the grocery store. You probably bought an actual chicken, either live or recently dead. If you were lucky, somebody had already plucked it and gutted it for you, but you might very well have to do those parts yourself before you got around to the actual cooking stage.

This smelled, if you'll forgive the pun, fairly foul. We think of kitchens as places that produce tasty aromas, but that's because the much less pleasant parts of the process are done off-site nowadays, and we have the technology to keep everything fresh until it's used. Which means, among other things, that there's much less risk of food-borne disease now for those who work in the kitchen, and those who eat its creations.

You also don't have to worry as much anymore about your kitchen destroying your home. "Did I leave the oven on?" is a proverbial worry, but how many times has your oven caught fire while you were in the house to deal with it? For most of us, never. But when food is being prepared in wood-burning stoves, ovens, and open hearths, the danger is ever-present—not to mention the risk of *people* being burned.

The solution to this might be to separate the kitchen from the house. That way the stinks of food preparation are kept away from the living quarters, and if anything catches fire, you have a better chance of keeping the destruction confined to that outbuilding. You do pay a price, though, and not only in the form of a separate building and the land to put it on; sometimes that means the food will arrive at table rather cooler and less appetizing than it ought to be, because you have to wrangle a bevy of servants to carry it through to where the diners are sitting.

For most people, though, it wasn't possible to have a separate kitchen—in either the "outbuilding" or "dedicated room" senses. Go back far enough in time, or look at the houses of the truly poor, and you find a one-room dwelling with a fire that serves the triple purposes of heat, light, and cooking. More than one fire means needing to gather at least twice as much fuel. (I don't actually know, but now that I type this I wonder, whether the rise of multiple hearths in a dwelling tracks at all to the use of coal instead of wood.) The earliest designs have a hole in the roof for smoke to (theoretically) escape through—and actually rely on that smoke to help keep the thatching free of bugs. Chimneys are a much later technology.

In those buildings, the kitchen is also the bedroom and the sitting room and everything else, because rooms with a dedicated single purpose are very much the domain of the wealthy—here defining "wealth" on a global and historical scale, i.e. including a great deal that we would call abject poverty nowadays. And in cities, your single room might not even have a fire, because that's pretty much just *asking* to burn the whole place down, and a good chunk of the city along with it.

So if you, gentle reader, live off of takeout and fast food and things otherwise not prepared at home, tell yourself that you're part of a long and respectable urban tradition. Why is "baker" a dedicated profession? Because relatively few people baked their own bread at any point in history, especially in cities. Many of them went out and bought it instead. You might buy all your food pre-prepared by someone else, from street-side stalls or carts that were the equivalent of modern food trucks, albeit with a much more limited selection. At home your larder would contain things like fruit, cheese, preserved meat, and bread rapidly going stale, i.e. things you could make a cold meal from.

(And then you'd have to deal with ants and rats and so forth, but I think vermin are going to need to be their own essay someday. Suffice it to say that if you ever find yourself thinking, "god, there are so many flies in my house," it almost certainly is nothing compared to the past. And now imagine trying to keep them from getting all over your food.)

This all changes in a futuristic society, of course—or one with prevalent enough magic to solve the problems that way. A microwave already cooks things without applying heat (or, if you want to be *really* pedantic, doesn't even cook them; it more or less causes dishes to cook themselves, by agitating the molecules such that they generate their own heat). Preserving food in cold and vermin-proof boxes opens up a lot of options; so does the ability to undo decay, either with localized time reversal or something like the D&D spell *purify food and drink*—though in that situation you're still temporarily putting up with the smell and unappetizing appearance of things that have gone bad.

Or you could conjure your food from thin air. In folklore it's a miracle; in science fiction it's more likely to be the product of some kind of "matter replicator" that can give you a ham sandwich or a perfect steaming cup of Earl Grey tea in the blink of an eye. (Which is to say, a miracle.) Maybe someday we'll have 3D meat printers in our houses that can assemble proteins and flavorings into whatever form of beef or chicken or fish you desire.

And when that happens, maybe we'll go back to not needing

kitchens. Just some kind of food-producing machine, and maybe one that makes things warm or cold if the food producer doesn't have those functions built in. But I suspect that people who enjoy cooking would find that to be a sad day indeed.

Dining Customs

To wrap up the topic of food for now, I'd like to talk about dining customs. When, where, and how we eat our meals are the kinds of things we take for granted, assuming that everyone does it more or less the same way—but of course that isn't true.

Let's start with "when." How many meals do you eat in a day? Three has become the standard for many of us...but it also depends on how you define a meal. In Britain, for example, you might have breakfast, lunch, tea, and then supper, with "tea" occupying an ambiguous zone between a meal and a snack. Hobbits famously eat six meals a day, when they can get them: breakfast, second breakfast, elevenses, luncheon, afternoon tea, and supper, at least according to one list I found. The less fortunate might get by on two, or even one.

The timing varies, too—to the point where we've coined words like "brunch" for a meal that lands in the disputed zone between breakfast and lunch. In eighteenth century England, five o'clock was a fashionably *late* hour for dinner; if you stayed up past sunset, you might have a lighter supper (not synonymous in those days with "dinner") later on. Given that I often work until two or three o'clock in the morning, I eat what Taco Bell has abominably dubbed "fourthmeal" around midnight, so I don't wind up going sixteen hours or more without food.

Which meal is the biggest one? For us sedentary types it's often the evening one; by contrast, farm folk might eat a much heartier breakfast to fuel themselves for a strenuous day. As for what goes in it, that varies widely by the time of day and part of the world. American breakfasts these days tend to be sweet, but if you stay in a European hotel you'll see a wide array of meats and cheeses among the baked goods and jam, and in Japan a traditional breakfast might include miso soup and fish. For non-vegetarians in the U.S., a dinner without animal protein might feel like it's lacking something, so ingrained is the "meat and side dish" model in our consciousness. Meanwhile, rice is fundamental enough to Japanese cuisine that the word for its cooked form also means "meal"—because without rice, have you really had a meal?

Then there's the question of how you eat it. In my household, when we're trying to pick a restaurant for dinner, we sometimes approach it by asking ourselves whether we're in a mood for forks, chopsticks, or just picking stuff up in our hands. (It sounds silly, but it helps narrow the field to certain types of cuisine.) Knives, spoons, and chopsticks are all ancient, but forks are a remarkably recent invention: as cooking utensils they've been around for a long time, but they didn't become popular for eating with until roughly the 10th century in the Middle East, the 14th century in Italy, and as late as the 18th century elsewhere in Europe and in the U.S. In some parts of the world you may not even use utensils at all, at least not of a durable kind: Ethiopian cuisine, for example, uses pieces of flatbread as an edible means of conveying food to the mouth.

How about where you have your meal? My husband and I bought a house last year, and for the first time in our adult lives, we have an actual table to eat at. Prior to that, our meals were set on tray tables or our laps, because the space the architect had intended to be our dining area was instead taken up by bookshelves. Larger houses (like the one I grew up in) may have a kitchen table for casual meals, and then a separate dining room for more formal events.

But sitting in a chair at a table is a very western model of doing things. In East Asia, you're traditionally more likely to be on a cushion on the floor—and these days restaurants may have a footwell underneath, as a concession to the decreased familiarity with kneeling. Formal banquets there didn't involve huge tables that seated dozens, but instead separate small tables for each diner, which could be added and taken away as needed. And then in fancy Roman society you weren't even sitting upright; you took your meals in *triclinia*, reclining on your left side as you ate.

Which brings us to handedness. Although left-handed people make up roughly ten percent of the population, many societies stigmatize the use of the left hand, especially in certain matters of etiquette—which includes eating. When the left hand is associated with cleaning oneself after defecation (as in Islam and other cultures), you can understand why eating with the right hand would be preferred.

And then, of course, dining customs can be used to express hierarchy. In Jackie Chan's autobiography, he mentions that the school he trained at served the eldest students first, with the platters working their way down the tables by order of seniority. The result was that the youngest students frequently got nothing but rice, all of the meat and vegetables having been taken by their superiors. The head of a household often gets the choicest cuts—or a guest does, if one is in attendance. And it's common for diners to hold off on starting their meal until the highest-ranking person present, whether that's the head of household, a guest, a boss, or the most senior member of an organization, has begun to eat.

Gender plays a role here, too. Even in our theoretically equal modern era, women often feel subconscious or overt pressure to order low-calorie meals or eat very daintily when in public, especially at major events—and then go home and devour something else to make up the deficit. In gender-segregated societies, women might not eat in the presence of men at all, taking their meals separately, often later, and perhaps from lesser options—echoing the hierarchy from Jackie Chan's school. (The same thing may apply to children.) By contrast, nineteenth-century European society had fairly strict etiquette about how to properly mix genders at formal meals, and gentlemen were expected to assist and defer to ladies in various respects.

So take a look around, the next time you have a casual breakfast with your family or dinner in a restaurant or a lunch banquet at some work event. What kinds of spoken and unspoken rules guide how you eat? How do they differ based on context? And how many of them have changed from how things were done in the past?

Phonology the Easy Way

I'm not likely to get too deep into the subject of conlanging—constructing languages—in this series. It can fill an entire book on its own (I have several on my shelf), and it rapidly gets eyeball-deep in grammatical concepts that are completely impenetrable to the layperson (is your language going to be nominative-accusative or ergative-absolutive?). If you want to know more about that kind of thing, I recommend you consult a suitably in-depth work by a specialist.

Instead I'm going to talk about my quick-and-dirty method of conlanging. Because the vast majority of the time, all you need is names—and while grammar can play a role in those, you can also get away without worrying about it, and the difference will be barely perceptible.

The secret is phonology.

...or maybe orthography, but for our purposes here the two are interlinked. Phonology = the sounds in the language. Orthography = how those sounds are written. And if you're consistent about those two things, and you use them to differentiate one culture from another, you instantly give your world a feeling of solidity and realism.

In the real world, if I mention Elizabeth Tudor, Diane du Poitiers, and Wu Zetian, you stand a very high chance of guessing that those ladies were English, French, and Chinese. Various factors can mess with this—immigration, colonialism, global trade, and so forth—but the underlying principle that different languages produce different kinds of names holds true. That's why, in the Memoirs of Lady Trent, I have characters with names like Galinke n Rumeme Gbori, Nour bint Ahmad, and Heali'i. Any single name on its own may not register as being distinctive, but as the data points pile up (Nour is joined by Husam ibn Ramiz, Abu Azali, al-Jelidah, and so forth), your reader will get a sense of what a typical Akhian name looks like, even though Akhia is a made-up place. And they'll know that wherever Gaetano Rossi is from, it's probably not there.

Conlang websites and instructional books call this a "naming language," and they give lots of advice on how to create one. But while you can pick which phonemes (sounds) you want your language to have and which you want to exclude and what laws should govern how they're used—e.g. "this language has R but not L and only allows voiced stops in word-initial positions"—as that example suggests, you still rapidly fall down the hole of needing to know some technical details about phonology.

This is why my quick-and-dirty method is to copy the phonology and romanized orthography of real-world languages. I have an embarrassing number of foreign-language dictionaries on my shelf, from the days before Google Translate; I browse the entries until I have a sense of what kinds of patterns are distinctive to that language, then start making up my own words in that style.

Of course there are pitfalls to this approach. You may, for example, accidentally recreate a real word. This is nigh-impossible to avoid in some languages; Japanese's consonant-vowel syllabic structure means that a huge number of two-syllable constructions will turn out to mean something—or probably several somethings, given the high frequency of homophones. I recommend checking your invented name against the dictionary before you commit to it, not necessarily to avoid all possible duplications, but to at least make sure you avoid anything embarrassing. Or you might not recreate a specific word, but inadvertently give your name the structure of a past tense verb or something else distinctive.

You're also limited to languages that use the Latin alphabet or else are frequently transliterated; many of the options on Google Translate come up in scripts I can't read, without even an audio option to let me hear how it sounds. And on a broader worldbuilding level, you risk creating cognitive dissonance in your reader's mind if you give a name like Connairt to someone whose culture looks more Zulu than Irish.

Depending on the language you look to for inspiration, you also run the risk of alienating your reader with something too "difficult." Aliette de Bodard has said that for her Aztec-set Obsidian and Blood series, she gave the characters much shorter names than they would have had in reality, because Acatl is much easier for Anglophone readers to manage than Mictlantecuhtli. I'm more willing than the average reader to tackle names unfamiliar to me, but even I choke on something like Kwakwaka'wakw; the indigenous languages of the Pacific Northwest are unrelated to anything I have even a passing familiarity with, giving me no foothold for parsing that name and figuring out how to pronounce it. There's a temptation to stick with "easy" things, by which I mean the phonology characteristic of Romance and Germanic languages, maybe some Slavic or Greek if you're feeling adventurous. Bantu languages? Dravidian languages? Mongolian? No way, man. Too weird.

...I hope the problems with that "too weird" reaction are reasonably obvious. Naming only with European phonology is a bit like writing only about white characters. The world is much richer and more complex than that, and we don't do ourselves any services by assuming that readers can't handle "funny-looking" names. I'm selective in how I construct things, to avoid chucking specific undigestible combos at my readers; *bhfaighidh* is a real Irish word, but asking the layperson to cope with that many lenited consonants at once would be a bit much. But that doesn't mean I haven't used Irish Gaelic-style names from time to time, and the same goes for the other languages from which I've taken my cues.

Which brings us to the final pitfall, and the reason I mentioned orthography above. That verb *bhfaighidh*? Depending on your dialect, it's pronounced like one of two English words: "we" or "why."

I am not kidding. The F vanishes, the BH is pronounced like a W, the GH is sort of swallowed and the DH is like a Y—but if you haven't studied Irish, there's no way you could guess that.

Letters and the sounds they represent don't stay the same between languages, especially when you consider specific combinations of them. Someone who has never heard French in their life will make something out of that "Poitiers" above, but it ain't gonna be how a Parisian might say it. I looked at Tibetan for some of the names in *Within the Sanctuary of Wings*, but didn't realize until far, far too late just how hilariously Tibetan outclasses English in the spelling/pronunciation mismatch department. (Their last spelling reform was in the ninth century.) The language you're looking at may include sounds (like the Welsh LL) that don't really exist in English, or make distinctions (like the difference between aspirated and unaspirated P, very important in Mandarin) that aren't tracked in this language. And even if *you* know how these things should be said, your reader very well may not, and they'll make up their own version.

But that last is true of any names you might use, up to and including real names from the real world. Being prepared to have readers mispronounce things is part of the job.

So while the quick-and-dirty method has its risks, I really do recommend it as a way of deciding how the names of your setting should look and sound. For me, it's become a core part of my worldbuilding, so that even when the cultures I'm inventing don't map very closely to real times and places, I still go "okay, these guys are going to have Sumerian-ish names, and hers is going to have Malay phonology, and then for that guy let's go with Icelandic." The result is that even in a city with people from many parts of the fictional world, the reader can tell, without me ever *telling* them, that the differences are there.

What's in a Name?

Continuing on from the discussion of phonology, I want to get into names—not how they sound, but how they're used.

When I'm reading, I see a huge number of invented worlds where everyone has a given name and a family name, in that order. It's the blandest, most invisible way to name a character, because it's the stripped-down form of the name style that most of you reading this essay probably have. And it doesn't require the author to think very much.

But if you look around the world, and especially through history, it isn't always that simple.

Let's start with the family name. Those aren't universal; there have been lots of times and places where people didn't have any kind of inherited moniker. Instead they had given names, and maybe some kind of descriptive epithet. Like, for example, their profession: John the tailor. (Who in later times would become John Taylor.) Or their parentage: James, Robert's son. (Later known as James Robertson.) Or place-names: Simon, who lives in the woods. (Simon Woods.) Or physical characteristics, behavioral tics, and various other quirks.

As you can tell, a lot of these got pressed into service as family names over time, losing their semantic meaning in the process; Jenny Robertson isn't a son and her father's name was Bill, but somewhere back in the family tree there was a Robert with a son, just as there was a tailor in the Taylor family. I believe Iceland is the final Western holdout for actual patronymics: Helga Sigurdsdottir's father is Sigurd Olafson, whose father was Olaf Thorvaldson, and so on up the chain, with the "family name" changing each generation. Many Arabic cultures also use patronymics, sometimes a whole string of them detailing multiple generations of the family tree; the Arabic traveler referred to as ibn Fadlan was more properly known as Ahmad ibn Fadlān ibn al-Abbās ibn Rāšid ibn Hammād.

Heading off in the other direction, sometimes people have more than one family name! Hyphenation has become more of a thing in the United States in recent decades, but it's long been common in Hispanic countries to have a double last name, drawing from both the father's and the mother's side.

Or the society groups people into larger clans and smaller families, with people bearing monikers from both; Gaius Julius Caesar was of the *gens Julia*, but specifically of the Caesar branch within that *gens*. You get an echo of this in certain periods of English literature, where the introduction of someone as Thomas Howeton is met with the query, "Of the Devonshire Howetons?" In these situations, the hereditary nature of the affiliation is of vital importance, because it marks the individual as belonging to a group—a sharp contrast to the epithet-based approach, which is focused on the characteristics that mark someone out individually.

Of course, societies often mix these things together with a semi-free hand. The cognomen or third part of the triple Roman name started out as an epithet instead of a hereditary marker (and when that shift happened, it got more common for Romans to have a fourth name—the agnomen—to pick up the nicknaming slack). Or your Roman might be referred to in a text as the son of his father, as a means of clarification. Someone in a patronymic culture might be much better known by their nickname than by their father's name.

But the mixture and the balance thereof can say quite a bit about the society: anybody who bothers to name their great-great-grandfather when introducing themselves is clearly quite invested in lineage as a thing of importance, while subdividing one's family within a clan implies key details of status or alliance that inhere to those groups. Having a matronymic, or name derived from one's mother, might indicate a matrilineal society—or it might mean your mother was unwed, and you therefore have no father's name to use—or your father died before you were born—or your mother was such a famous badass that you decided to commemorate her; the children of Empress Matilda sometimes used the name FitzEmpress (the most famous of these being the eventual king, Henry II).

Then there's the given name…or more than one. Many of you reading this probably have a middle name, which in the United States is a term that encompasses pretty much anything that might come between the given name and the family name: the second part of a two-part name, maiden names, patronymics, etc. These reflect a broad swath of naming conventions being fit, Procrustes-like, into the model of the "American name."

Or many people wind up with multiple given names, possibly to honor a slew of relatives on both sides of the family, possibly because the parents couldn't make up their minds. The children of immigrants frequently have "American" first names and "ethnic" middle names (or the other way around), reflecting their parents' double desire to have their children fit in but also maintain a tie to their ancestral culture. And some of us—myself included—have middle names just because that's what you *do* in this country. It serves no practical function, apart from being a second canvas upon which the parents can exercise their creativity.

On top of that, you may have a religious name! My husband has both a middle name and a baptismal name—the latter of which doesn't appear in official government documentation, but he was baptized Catholic, and neither his given nor middle names come from recognized saints, so his grandmother had to choose something in a hurry when the priest made his disapproval clear. Jews may have a *shem hadokesh* for use in formal religious documents; Wiccans and neopagans may choose names for ritual contexts, separate from what they call themselves in daily life. Likely the same is true for other religions I'm less familiar with. Whether the religious name is considered to have magical power or is merely a way of marking the boundary between the sacred and the secular, it's yet another layer in the pile of monikers a single individual might carry.

And when *that's* all said and done, there's the question of what order you put the names in. In the West, it's usually personal name followed by family, while in East Asia—and, randomly, in Hungary—it's the other way around. I've heard this attributed to the individual vs. communal mentalities of those respective regions, but I think it may have as much or more to do with grammar (whether modifiers precede or follow the word they modify). Where fiction is concerned, I'm not sure I've ever seen the family name come first outside of settings that are obviously meant to be direct analogues of East Asia, just as I haven't seen double family names very often, or any of the other variations that exist across the world. 95% of the time, it's one given name, one family name, the end.

I'd like to see more authors shake that up.

Names and Their Meaning

I originally thought I would get through the topic of names in a single essay. (More fool me.) Let's move on to what names *mean*.

On the wall of my office I have a laminated map called the Atlas of True Names, which labels the world with our best guesses at what all the place names mean—because nearly every name in the world originally meant something, before it went through the rock tumbler of time and linguistic change.

Let's use my own name as an example of what I mean. "Marie" is the French form of what in English would be "Mary," and if you trace them back through the Latin Maria to the Greek Mariam you get to the Hebrew Miryam, which means…well, Wikipedia gives options including "rebellion", "bitter sea", "strong waters", "mistress", "exalted one", "ruling one", "wished for child", "beautiful," "beloved," and I could keep going but I won't. "Brennan" is the Anglicized form of two different Irish surnames, Ó Braonáin and Ó Branáin, with the Ó indicating a descendant, Braonáin meaning "moisture" or "drop," and Branáin meaning "little raven." We could play this game all day—but in practical terms, the only time people in the U.S. pay much attention to the buried meaning is when they're naming their kid. The fact that you could translate my name as "beautiful drop" or "bitter little raven" is not only irrelevant, it requires a fair bit of effort to uncover.

With other names, though, the semantic meaning is obvious.

Surnames like Baker, place names like Meadowcreek, given names like Rose or Amber or Heather. For women with English-language names it's lots of flowers (Lily) and gems (Ruby) and virtues (Grace) and so forth. When men have names like that, they're often repurposed occupational surnames like Carter or Hunter (which have been going unisex in recent years), or they veer in the direction of what always sound to me like stereotypical romance-hero names, such as Blaze or Cliff.

In a language written with logograms, the semantic meaning is visible all the time—but, perhaps because of that, people may not place as much emphasis on it. In Japan, where most (though not all) names are written with Chinese characters, parents often choose on the basis of sound rather than concerning themselves much with the meaning of the characters used. In a story I'm working on, the Japanese-American protagonist is named Mika, written with the kanji for "summer sea"...but her name could as easily be composed of "say perfume," "outlook song," or "tree trunk addition."

And then you've got the stereotypical image of "Native American names"—things like Sitting Bull, Touch the Clouds, Crazy Horse (or rather, His Horse is Crazy), etc, where the name is composed of an entire meaningful phrase, rendered in English. (In looking up examples of this, I found what may be my favorite, which is "They Are Afraid of Her." That was Crazy Horse's daughter.) This extends to Mesoamerica, too, with names like Feather Skull or Jaguar Paw. Sometimes Chinese names in fiction are rendered in a similar fashion, which annoys the snot out of some Chinese-Americans I know. This type of name may crop up among Wiccans and neopagans, though it's frequently rendered as a compound word instead of a phrase; you also get that in fantasy, whether it's *Elfquest* (Clearbrook), Mercedes Lackey's Hawkbrothers (Firesong), or some other example.

Overall, my impression is that fantasy and science fiction generally drift to one end or the other of this spectrum, but rarely make use of the middle. Assuming that the story doesn't use real-world names (which, by their nature, partake of several points along the spectrum), you either get names composed of interesting English words, or invented names whose presumed etymological underpinnings are never specified. I can't even think of many patronymics, whether they take the form of the English "-son" suffix or some other recurrent element. You also don't tend to see the nobiliary particles that crop up in many European names, like the Slavic *-ski/-sky/-cki*, the German *von* or *zu*, or the French *de/du/d'/des*, marking the estate of an aristocrat or aristocratic progenitor. Basically, a lot of names in speculative fiction are random collections of syllables, with little or no thought given to how they got put together.

Or to where they came from. One of the great failures of worldbuilding in Robert Jordan's Wheel of Time series can be found in the country of Andor. Despite having a proud tradition of female rulership stretching back to the founding queen Ishara, we do not meet one single Andoran woman named Ishara or any variant thereof. (The Wheel of Time wiki tells me there is one other woman named Ishara mentioned in the entire series, but she's a historical figure who died centuries before the founding of Andor.)

This? Is pretty damn implausible. While occasionally there are name taboos, it's much more common for the names of famous people to get reused in various forms, whether those are kings and queens or religious figures (saints, anybody?) or great heroes of the past. Heck, names in general get reused a lot: my poor copy-editor for the Onyx Court series was forever querying whether Edward Grenville was an error and I meant Edward Fitzwilliam, etc. Henry VIII came within an inch of naming his second daughter Mary, *just like his first daughter*, before he decided she should be Elizabeth instead. We tend to avoid this in fiction because it's confusing for the reader, but you can have nicknames and variants on the same name— Elizabeth, Beth, Bess, Liz, Liza, Lizzy, Eliza, Elspeth, Isabel, Elise, and countless more—which gives a sense of realism and connectedness.

In fact, if you want to write about some real-world cultures or fictional iterations thereof, a certain amount of name repetition comes with the territory. In Japanese, for example, it used to be common to see the name of a son use the first half (i.e. first character) of his father's name, so that Oda Nobunaga's sons were Nobutada, Nobukatsu, Nobutaka, and so forth, while his father was Nobuhide. I recently watched the Chinese drama *Nirvana in Fire*, where the sons of the Emperor have the given names Jingyu, Jingyan, Jinghuan, Jingxuan, etc. This is the concept of the generation name at work: a syllable shared by each member of a generation, usually drawn from a "generation poem" that tells you which character to use for the next round of kids.

On the one hand, this can be bloody confusing for the audience, because of the high degree of name similarity it spawns. (Heck, there are authors who recommend you avoid using even the same first *letter* more than once per story if you can avoid it, at least for major characters.) On the other hand, a practice like that can add depth to the setting, showing the connection between members of a given generation and the sense of continuity with previous generations—and even, for those writers willing to assay poetry, adding a narrative dimension in the form of the generation poem from which the names are drawn.

Just as the stripped-down given name + family name approach misses the opportunity for variety and flavor, so too does the "random collection of syllables" approach. You don't need to be writing about China to give your heroine something like a generation name, and I would pay cash money to see a science fiction writer give their space-faring characters names like Quasarshine or Seeks the Galactic Center. Marking out your aristocrats with a nobiliary particle will help the reader distinguish between them and the common-born people in the story, and inventing a patronymic suffix will create a sense that "family name" is a different structural ballgame from "given name," but not an unrelated one.

...yeah, I'm not finishing this topic in two essays, either. Let's continue on to how the name get used!

The Etiquette of Names

The etiquette of when and how names get used is something I think Americans sometimes have trouble grasping, because our society has jettisoned a huge percentage of those customs. The speed with which we get on a first-name basis with one another is shocking by historical standards—assuming we don't start there right out of the gate. (Writing this essay, I realized I don't even know my neighbors' last names, because we all introduced ourselves with first names only.) In many cases, the only gradation of formality we mark is whether you call someone by their actual given name, or by a less formal nickname.

But in many times and places, including various parts of the world today, the given name is reserved for people with whom one is on fairly intimate terms: family members, *maybe* very close friends. For everyone else, or in non-private situations, you use something else.

In some cases this will still be their name, just a different component thereof. Where there are multiple given names, one may be for private use (for example, a childhood name), the other for public (the name taken at adulthood). If the society has family names, those commonly get used for more formal modes of interaction.

The difference between forms of address can convey a host of social cues that get lost if there's no etiquette of names: two friends or sweethearts moving to a first-name basis is a watershed of intimacy, while a social superior calling an inferior by their given name can be a way of asserting their power. Meanwhile, a close companion suddenly addressing you by your family name could herald a sudden gulf of distance or hostility, while in a more hierarchical context it might be a way of conveying respect. (In the movie *Hidden Figures*, it's a huge moment when the white manager finally addresses her black employee as Mrs. Vaughan, instead of Dorothy.)

Names often don't operate on their own, either. In English men are formally addressed as mister/Mr., a term derived from "master." The female equivalent was "mistress," but over time it bifurcated into Miss and Mrs., the former indicating an unmarried woman, the latter a married one—a distinction that never got made for men. Ms., derived from the same source, formerly enjoyed scattered usage as a way to address a woman whose marital status was unknown, but now it's acquired currency as a way of ditching that question entirely. Several European languages follow a similar pattern (*señor/señorita/ señora*; *monsieur/mademoiselle/madame*; *Herr/Fräulein/Frau*)—I do not know of any that mark the marital status of men, but that would be an interesting detail to add to a fictional world!

Other forms of address differentiate based on rank. As the "master"/"mistress" example implies, even today's routine etiquette has its origins in those gradations; "sir" and "madam," which we now deploy to be polite to anybody, used to be much more restrictive. (But don't get confused; "sirrah" was used for *inferiors*, not equals or superiors.) In Japanese neither marital condition nor gender factor in—men and women alike are *-san* in basic address—but there's a host of other honorifics that mark status, like *-sama* (formerly used for lords; now used much more widely to convey deference), *-sensei* (not "teacher" so much as a term of respect that gets used for teachers, doctors, and other noteworthy figures), *-senpai* (a senior student or someone in a comparable position to you), all the positional titles within a company, and more.

Going back to English, there's a whole complex framework of etiquette around addressing nobility of different ranks: this one is a "my lord" or "your lordship," but that one is "your

Excellency" and this other one is "your Grace." Ascribed virtues take the place of names. Furthermore, personal names often vanish in that context, replaced instead by estate names; William Cavendish, the Marquess of Hartington, could be addressed and referred to as Lord Hartington. Even to his good friends, he might just be Hartington, or possibly Cavendish, but rarely if ever William, Will, or Bill—at least to anyone other than his immediate family members.

Speaking of family, sometimes that can also take the place of names. Many cultures around the world eschew the use of personal names within a family, seeing it as more respectful to use kinship terms. In English we do that a little bit; very few of us call our parents by their names, and if a grandparent's or aunt's/uncle's name gets used, it's usually prefaced by the appropriate term: Grandma Nell, Uncle Fred.

But extensions of that principle which sound natural in other languages—younger sister, elder brother, second cousin, etc—sound clunky in English because we don't have specific terms for those relationships, only adjectives we can tack on when we need to make distinctions. Then there's Arabic, where an adult may be addressed as the father or mother of their child (Abu Mazen/Umm Mazen). And, of course, kinship terms can be used as honorifics, their literal meaning discarded; in some societies any elderly man or woman is a grandfather or grandmother to a respectful stranger, and sometimes the middle-aged are similarly aunts and uncles.

Trying to replicate these shifts and nuances in fiction can lead to difficulty, it's true. When I first picked up Dorothy Dunnett's historical novel *The Game of Kings*, it took me a while to really internalize that Lymond, Mr. Crawford, Francis, and the Master of Culter were all the same person. (Estate name, family name, given name, and title as heir to the Barony of Culter.) But the flip side is that once I *had* internalized it, the shifts between those names added power to the story: someone referring to the protagonist as Francis was as good as shooting off a rocket to signal that the character speaking had a particular relationship to him. The intimacy of a nickname (which I understand figures *heavily* in Russian literature), the formality of a title, the reminders of familial structure encoded in a kinship term—those all add to the story.

So while including them creates a variety of challenges, I'm in favor of more people tackling those challenges, figuring out how to present them so the reader gets trained in the necessary habits of thinking. Even the basic etiquette of given name vs. family name + title is something we see very little of anymore.

Greetings and Respect

Much like the etiquette of names, the etiquette of greeting and showing respect has massively atrophied in the United States. In a society where everyone is equal (at least in principle), we devote much less concern to marking other people out as worthy of particular courtesy. But for a great many of the societies we write about, there's enough hierarchy for this to be a fairly big deal. In fact, screwing up—whether deliberately or on accident—can get one into degrees of trouble ranging from public reprimand to dueling to execution.

I'm always leery of declaring anything "universal," because human culture varies so widely through place and time. But if there's a single principle on this topic that I think deserves that label, it's the idea that height = power. Therefore, lowering oneself in some fashion is a sign of humility or respect. Bowing (whether European-style or Asian) is one method of lowering the head; curtsying is the skirts variation. Kneeling takes you deeper, and prostration is the end-point of this spectrum, short of digging a hole to put yourself in. Touching or gesturing toward the feet of an elder is common in India; I've seen it explained not just as a lowering gesture, but as a way of saying the person is so worthy of reverence, even to touch the dust on their feet is an honor.

Looking at this principle from the other direction, putting someone on a throne or dais asserts their status by physically raising them above everyone else. During my first year of grad school, when I couldn't turn Anthropology Brain off for love or money, I found myself noting the different architectural styles of the two throne rooms in Disney's 1959 film *Sleeping Beauty*: the good king and queen can be approached in a straight line and are only one or two small steps above their subjects, but Maleficent rules from a high platform that can only be reached via staircases to the side. Did the animators consciously think through the implications of that? I have no idea. But the subconscious impression was likely there, regardless.

Saluting is one of the few hierarchical gestures that still survives in the United States, primarily in a military context. Some historians explain this by referencing medieval armor, saying the gesture evolved out of knights raising their visors to show their faces. Whether or not that's true, it almost certainly also has a connection to the social etiquette of hats, which lower-class men were expected to remove when in the presence of their superiors. Over time, this became a simple lifting of the hat, or merely touching it, or gesturing to a hat that is no longer there. Tugging one's forelock may be a related gesture. But conversely, women's etiquette said to keep your head covered—which is why "Sunday hats" linger in some parts of society that have given up on headgear everywhere outside of church.

Not all greetings are about showing respect to a higher-status individual. Some of them are instead about showing friendliness—which goes back to the visor-raising theory. Why do we shake hands with the right hand? Partly because the left hand has often been considered dirty (in some cultures it's used for sanitary tasks), but there's also a theory that it communicates non-hostility; given that the majority of people are right-handed, occupying that side with a handshake is a way of saying "I'm not holding a weapon and I'm not likely to draw one right this second." Since shaking hands requires you to get very close to the other person, you can see where that might be a concern.

Kissing also indicates friendliness, whether it's on the mouth (as in the kiss of peace—not the best for avoiding communicable disease) or, more commonly, on the cheek (as in many parts of Europe, with regional variations ad infinitum). Kissing the hand is an interesting case: in religious or historical aristocratic contexts, the idea was to kiss someone's signet ring, a symbol of their power, but in a cross-gender context, it's startlingly intimate, especially depending on where the gentleman puts his lips. Good manners in one context might be an unacceptable invasion of personal space in another.

These things get really interesting when you look at the ideas underpinning them. Reading the *Mahabharata* recently, I came across repeated instances of *pradakshina* (or *parikrama*), aka circumambulation; looking it up, I came across a story that when the goddess Parvati told her two sons to go around the world to gain knowledge, the younger son, Ganesha, walked a circle around Parvati and declared that she contained the world. The *anjali mudra*, pressing the palms together as an accompaniment to or stand-in for the word "namaste," can position the hands at several different heights, corresponding to different chakras in the body, which brings in a host of potential meanings. The *hongi*, the Maori practice of pressing your nose and forehead to someone else's, is a way of exchanging the breath of life, which connects you to the other person (and bestows some obligations, too).

People aren't the only targets of these signals. Those instances of *pradakshina* in the *Mahabharata* are sometimes directed at weapons or chariots; Catholics may kneel to the altar in a church before taking a seat in a pew. I bow when entering or leaving the main floor at my karate dojo, which helps to mark off that space as special—a realm where particular behaviors and rules apply, materially different from the waiting room beyond the edge of the mat. Whether it's removing a hat or bestowing a kiss, nearly any gesture of respect that can be directed at a person can also go to an object, if it carries enough significance.

If you're writing spec fic, you can make up nearly anything and say it's how a particular culture greets people and shows respect. In Tamora Pierce's novel *Lioness Rampant*, for example, the Doi cover their eyes. But it can't be random: if it isn't familiar to the reader, you need to make sure the text conveys the underlying logic, or else it will feel very artificial.

Gestures of Contempt

So we've been talking about etiquette and how different cultures convey respect, or at least convey the expectation that respect will be given.

...but sometimes, what you really want is for your characters to be horrifically rude to one another.

As with words, gestures of contempt are powered more by intent than by inherent meaning. A gesture that's innocuous or even respectful in one culture might be a grave insult in another—and in fact, you can potentially turn the former into the latter by performing it insincerely. They say in social justice discussions that intent is not magic; if I accidentally do something offensive, the fact that I didn't mean to doesn't erase that moment of shock and hurt. But intent does still say something about the person responsible, and when it comes to cross-cultural ideas of vulgar behavior, it's often the main factor making one gesture totally crass while another is nothing special.

Take the middle finger. In a lot of Western countries, extending it while folding the other fingers is a non-verbal insult. But not in all cases; some people will use that instead of the index finger when pointing at something on a page. Directionality makes a difference to how the gesture is interpreted. Similarly, I was once telling a story to a pair of Brits over dinner and held up my index and middle fingers to indicate two of something—whereupon one of the Brits reached across the table and turned my hand around so my palm was facing outward, not inward. I had forgotten that the V-sign with an inward palm is the British equivalent of the middle finger. It's a tiny difference, but one that matters.

If you go digging for some underlying meaning to explain why these things are offensive, it can often be difficult to find. The middle finger, being (usually) the longest of the set, has a long and storied history of representing the phallus, which goes some way toward explaining why it has a vulgar connotation; it's also associated with magic for the same reason. The OK sign, with the index finger and thumb forming a circle, also has offensive meaning in some places because of sexual implications—but in Arabic countries it's a sign of the evil eye instead.

And why the V-sign? The old tale that it dates back to the medieval wars between England and France, with the French cutting two fingers off captured English longbowmen to prevent them from using their weapons again, doesn't hold water. (They cut off three fingers, not two, and the gesture is probably a lot more recent than some medieval Englishman saying "screw you; I can still shoot" anyway.) Or take the euphemistically named *bras d'honneur*, the "arm of honor," where you raise one fist (again with the palm inward) and slap that biceps with your other hand. Is that a symbolic threat, saying you're going to punch them? We don't know.

In fact, I sometimes think that nearly any hand position can be taken as offensive, if there's a cultural belief backing it. Forming a fist with your thumb between your index and middle fingers? In the United States you're pretending you stole someone's nose or signaling the letter T in the manual alphabet...but in Italy that used to be called the "fig sign," and it represented female genitalia. Spreading all your fingers and, in a reversal of the usual pattern, turning your palm toward somebody else? You might be waving, or doing jazz hands—but if you're in Greece that's the *mountza*, and it has the connotation of a curse. Even more so if you do it with both hands, one stacked behind the other. (Apparently if you want to signal "five" in Greece, it's safer to turn your palm inward, reversing my "two" mistake described above.) In the Mediterranean and Latin America, the "sign of the horns," with the index and pinkie fingers extended, makes use of both directions; swiveling back and forth is a way of indicating that someone is a cuckold.

What fascinates me is how many of these things carry a double meaning. Go back further in Italian history to ancient Rome, and the sign of the fig was used to ward off evil spirits. This isn't incompatible with the anatomical symbolism; both male and female genitalia have been used to scare away demons or ill fortune, and in Irish mythology the women of Emain disrupt Cu Chulainn's battle frenzy by flashing their breasts at him.

Some vulgar gestures have a clear antecedent, though. Looking to the Middle East again, we find that shoes and the soles of the feet are considered dirty (quite sensibly so), which means that showing them to someone is an insult. Remember all those Iraqis hitting the statue of Saddam Hussein with their shoes? That was a massive, public display of contempt. Therefore, sitting with one foot across the other knee, or with your feet outstretched, is one of the ways Westerners often give accidental offense to Arabs. Similarly, quite a lot of cultures associate the left hand with either evil or sanitary purposes, which means that handing something over or receiving it with the left hand alone is crass.

In fiction, you can sell just about anything as contemptuous so long as the characters react to it appropriately. You can give it a cultural underpinning if you want; the story about longbows and the V-sign may not be true in reality, but in fiction something along those lines could be a great touch of historical depth. In many cases, though, trying to explain why the gesture is offensive would probably turn into an unnecessary infodump. Instead it can be like the line from Shakespeare: "Do you bite your thumb at me, sir?" We don't need to know why biting the thumb is an insult for it to work in the scene. We only need to know whether this is a mild way of saying "screw you" or something to fight a duel over, whether it's merely vulgar or a sign that the other person is placing a curse. The intent and the reaction will tell us all that's necessary.

Insults

Content note: by dint of the subject matter, this essay is going to contain a number of offensive words.

You can learn a lot about a society by looking at what they consider to be insulting.

The basic principle is pretty simple: if you want to speak negatively about a person, you ascribe to them qualities you consider to be undesirable. Or—as a corollary—it isn't so much the qualities as the way they're spun; the same action might be described as courageous if you approve of it, reckless if you don't. (I've always found it interesting that *sangfroid* is a good thing to have, but being cold-blooded is bad…even though those literally mean the same thing.) So when you're trying to decide how to insult a character, the question is what the speaker considers to be bad, and how the target's behavior can be framed in those terms.

There are patterns in how this tends to play out. One is stupidity: even in the current anti-intellectual climate of the United States, we generally agree that being stupid is not good. Because of the blurred line between this and outright mental disability, stupidity has been on the euphemism treadmill for literally centuries, as we bring in a never-ending series of new, theoretically neutral terms for disability, which then become all-purpose insults. Fool, dunce, moron, cretin, imbecile, retard— the list goes on and on. "Cretin" is not derived from an ethnic insult for people from Crete, as I once saw a blog post suggest; it's from the French *chrétien*, "Christian." And not because "Christian" was an insult: on the contrary, it was used to distinguish human beings from brute animals, so calling a disabled person a Christian was supposed to remind you of your shared humanity. (Unfortunately, it didn't work.)

Speaking of brute animals, that's another common way to insult someone. Many languages use the qualities of animals both as praise and as condemnation, depending on the quality in question. In English, you can insult a woman (or these days, a man) by calling them a bitch, a female dog; in Spanish it's *zorra* instead, i.e. a vixen, a female fox. In Japanese, *chikushō* or "beast" is kind of an all-purpose swear word. Being cold-blooded likens you to a reptile, which is off-putting to our mammalian biases. The Chinese zodiac may promote the admirable qualities of the pig, but in English calling someone by that name is not a compliment—I wonder, but don't know, whether this is especially true among religious groups where pork is considered unclean.

I also wonder if animal-based insults are less common in cultures that occupy a less dominant and distanced position over the natural world. Or maybe they're more common, because those people, being intimately familiar with animal behavior, know exactly when you're acting like the worst of them. Seeing which animals get singled out for metaphorical use, whether positive or negative, fills in a whole realm of symbolic thinking for that culture.

Going back to "bitch," gender is an unfortunately common source of derogatory terms. When women are considered to be inferior, one of the worst things you can do to a man is to compare him to a woman. Conversely, a woman who acts too much like a man will find herself insulted on those grounds instead. "Bitch" is notably versatile in this regard: when applied to a female target, it usually means she's being too strident, aggressive, etc., i.e. the negative version of what in a man would be considered confident and assertive behavior. But when applied to a male target, it usually implies weakness, lack of spine, and other supposedly womanish qualities. If you're trying to depict a society without strict gender roles and their associated chauvinism, therefore, it helps to scrutinize your language for these kinds of gender-skewed idioms and scrub them out.

This rapidly slides into matters of the body, as sex-specific characteristics become synecdoche for the whole. A man you don't like might be a dick or a prick, even though we have other aspects of our culture that valorize the male body. The female equivalents tend to carry more negative weight: pussy, cunt, etc. On the other hand, that latter word has a degree of general usage in British slang that's unthinkable in the U.S., while the former has recently been repurposed in American politics via the "pussy hat" phenomenon and "Pussy Grabs Back." Nobody's yet stood up for the word "asshole," though (despite the fact that, as the saying goes, assholes are like opinions: everybody has one. Or rather, the other way around). Until we start having conversations with sentient dung beetles, I'm pretty sure that everything associated with defecation is going to remain conceptually unclean and therefore fair game for insulting use.

Sexual behavior is a whole field of its own where this is concerned. Here gender comes right back in: a man who sleeps around might be a stud (good), but a woman who does the same is often a slut (bad). Harlot, whore, skank—again, the list goes on and on. Men more often get hit from the angle of homosexuality, which has seen a whole lot of reclamation effort in recent years, where U.S. parlance is concerned. Gay, fag/faggot, queer, fairy, and other such terms have been embraced by the LGBTQ movement, though others have fallen almost completely out of use (e.g. molly or nancy) and some are still right out (tranny for a trans person). And then there's the product of certain kinds of sexual behavior: calling someone a bastard no longer carries the connotation of illegitimate birth, but that was its origin, and as such it used to be grounds for a duel.

And then we have the racial, religious, and national slurs, which are unfortunately endless. The euphemism treadmill has been busily turning for people of African descent in the United

States; the NAACP is a prestigious organization, but using the phrase "colored people" these days is unacceptable, while "people of color" (whose meaning is broader) has been gaining currency.

Lots of these terms came into use when we were at war with a certain country and then faded after the war ended, because they reflect the political tensions of the time—so the ones that are still around are a good pointer to where those tensions are alive and well. Then they serve double duty, because you can insult someone not of that group by calling them an X-lover or other such pejorative. A few of them gained wider use along the way: saying that someone "gypped" you is a reference to the supposed dishonesty of gypsies, the people more properly known as Romani, while "welching" or "welshing" on a bet is possibly an artifact of the perception that Welsh people were likewise dishonest, and "jewing" indicates driving a hard bargain or even cheating.

The ones that really interest me in secondary worlds, though, are the terms that are really specific to their culture. References to great traitors of the past (as "Judas" is still used sometimes today) give you a sense of history's ongoing weight, if the reader has some context for the term. A really militarized society might use words like "civilian" as a way of sneering at people who don't contribute enough to the war effort. In the comic book series *Elfquest*, the hunter-gatherer Wolfriders' ultimate expression of condemnation is "meat to be wasted"—a person so contemptible they don't even deserve to play a final role in the food chain. These types of things take work to invent, and more work to sell the reader on the offensiveness of the term...but when done right, they make a vivid contribution to the mental landscape of the setting.

Profanity

Content note: by dint of the subject matter, this post is going to contain a number of offensive words.

As with our discussion of insults, there are a lot of foul words here. But I find it interesting that, at least in the modern United States, many of us would consider them far less offensive than some of the slurs from the previous essay—because the words traditionally considered "profanity" have spread through mainstream discourse, losing much of their power to shock along the way, while pejorative terms for groups marked by ethnic, religious, sexual, or gender difference have become increasingly unacceptable in polite conversation.

And you know what? I'm okay with that.

Here again there are patterns in what's considered to be profane (in the "offensive" rather than "not sacred" sense). In English, the two main sources of vulgar language are religion, and matters of the body.

On the religious side, we have "hell" and "damn." Profanity is also sometimes referred to as curse words, and that sense is very clear here; if you damn someone to hell, you are literally attempting to curse them. Some people also consider "Jesus Christ" and "God" to be off-limits, because of the prohibition against taking the Lord's name in vain. That mentality has been fading over time, though, and most of our other religious swearing has become so obsolete as to sound quaint: "Zounds!" is a shortening of "God's wounds," i.e. the wounds suffered by Christ, but few people can take that seriously these days. Ditto "gadzooks," which used to be "God's hooks," the nails used in the crucifixion, and "'sblood," "God's blood." The very British-sounding intensifier "bloody" may or may not have a connection to that last one; how offensive it is today depends on who you ask.

Blood leads us to the body and our other source of swearing, mostly via excrement and sex. A lot of the charge around obscene words come from the violation of taboos: you aren't supposed to talk about bodily waste, so "shit" and "piss" and "ass/arse" are shocking. (And if you don't want to be shocking, you retreat to euphemisms like "water" or much more academic terminology like "feces" and "urine"—which, because of how English developed, are Latinate instead of earthy Anglo-Saxon.) You also aren't supposed to talk about sex, so "fuck" is similarly charged. "Sodding," another word associated with British English more than American, is shortened from "sodomize," which puts it alongside "bugger" in the categorization of our curses.

But this varies from language to language. In the last essay I mentioned the Japanese *chikushō* or "beast," which is used as an expletive much like we might say "shit!" or "damn!" when something goes wrong. In English you might say something is beastly, but it isn't quite the same thing. Dennis Tedlock's book of Zuni narrative poetry, *Finding the Center*, leaves the archaic words *tísshomahhá* and *hanáhha* untranslated, saying "they have no meanings other than the emotions they are supposed to express," explicitly contrasting them with the religious and bodily references of English interjections. I'd love to find examples from other languages, especially from outside the sphere of long-term Christian influence—are there clusters of swear words that arise from different conceptual sources?

Speculative fiction has a long history of trying to come up with invented substitutes for standard English profanity. Some of these are obvious swaps, often done to get around TV restrictions on language: *Farscape*'s "frell" or *Battlestar Galactica*'s "frak" are pretty transparent. I have to admit I find "frell" unconvincing, simply because it sounds so *pretty*. In English most of our swearing comes from Germanic roots, which gives it a certain sound; "frell" is too light and liquid to pass. "Frak," on the other hand, has that hard stop at the end, which makes it sound more like profanity to me. C.S. Friedman's Coldfire Trilogy subs in "vulk," which is more than a random set of phonemes: the planet the series takes place on is extremely seismically active, so that earthquakes and volcanic activity are a constant threat. Since the planet was settled by colonists from Earth, it makes sense that the volcano/vulcanology root would give rise to "vulking" as a curse word.

On the religious end of things, sometimes I think you can't throw a rock at epic fantasy without hitting an oath built on the structure of "[god]'s [noun]"—where the noun is usually either a body part or an iconic object. As the examples above show, that's not unrealistic, but it does get predictable and tedious after a while. The Wheel of Time associates good with lightness and evil with darkness, which has problematic connotations I'll get into at some point, but it also gives rise to some setting-specific forms of swearing: light = fire, so while "Light!" is a socially acceptable interjection, "burn me" and "ashes" are considered much more vulgar. In a world where floods are a frequent problem, maybe water-based terminology would become a source of oaths. Decay has mild usage in English, via "rot," but you could build more on that principle; ditto the closely-related issue of disease.

But in the end, the challenge here isn't to come up with a new swear word; it's to convince the reader of the weight that word carries. In Mary Gentle's Book of Ash series, she has her present-day historian translate medieval profanity into modern idiom, because he knows the originals won't have the right impact on his readers. To really convey the sense of transgression, you need everything around it in the story to reflect that. If your viewpoint character doesn't normally use such language, have them flinch from it. If the speaker is normally much better-mannered, acknowledge how much of a breach this is. Think of whatever you consider to be a truly offensive word, think of how you would write about that word coming up in your own daily life—and then make it that shocking in the story, too.

Idioms and Slang

Slang is an incredibly tricky topic in fiction, including stuff set in the real world. Used correctly, it can be powerful tool for vividly evoking a sense of place, time, and class: a common Brooklyn laborer in 1950 and a rich California teenager in 1980 are going to use *wildly* different idioms in their casual speech. But used incorrectly…I once bounced right out of a Regency-set fantasy novel whose heroine talked like a character from *Buffy the Vampire Slayer*, because it kept undermining my sense of the setting.

Not every novel has to precisely replicate the speech of its era, of course; that's a very specific game, and not one every story is interested in playing. Like the movie *A Knight's Tale* opening with its medieval peasants singing "We Will Rock You" at a joust, you can advertise up front that your goal is to create a different effect entirely. But not every writer has the chops to pull that off, and when they fail, it falls very flat indeed.

But what about secondary-world fiction? The game there is even more complicated. Most of us attempt to write "neutral" prose, avoiding obvious markers of our time period. Nobody in a 1980s Tolkien clone ever said "radical, dude." (At least not that I'm aware of, and now I find myself really wanting to know if that *does* exist. Portal fantasies don't count.)

I say "attempt" because the illusion of neutrality is just that: an illusion. Everything about how we talk and write is tinged with the flavor of one era or another, and if you don't make a concerted effort to ensure the era in question is a different one, it will probably be identifiable decades later as belonging very much to the 1980s or the early 2000s or whenever. This pervades the text on a level down to the sentence structure and punctuation: after five years of writing the Memoirs of Lady Trent, I'm still in the process of scrubbing the Victorian influence out of my prose, and if you look at these blog essays you'll find them peppered with colons and semicolons and other markers of nineteenth-century diction. (Seriously, I can't get rid of them. I've tried.)

Let's leave behind the nitty-gritty bits like punctuation, though, and look at idioms more generally. What kinds of speech do we put in the mouths of our characters, and how can that help (or hinder) the worldbuilding?

Going back to Tolkien clones for a moment...the use of cod-medieval English in a certain type of epic fantasy used to be so widespread that we even have a slang term for *that*, saying the characters are speaking "forsoothly." Most of the writers who attempted to do this lacked Tolkien's ear for the rhythms of such speech, or even basic knowledge of its rules, which is why this is so easily parodied. If you're going to imitate the diction of a historical period, you need to immerse yourself in real examples, or else stick with that "neutral" prose; the latter is way less distracting than a bad attempt at the former.

As a result, you find very little "forsoothly" speech in most modern fantasy, even when the setting is meant to be more or less European-medieval. In fact, you're more likely to see the opposite: a certain flavor of "gritty," profanity-laden, modern-style language, meant to strip away the nostalgic haze that used to overlay such depictions. As a corrective I see why it happened, and it can be done well; on the other hand, after a while it becomes every bit as predictable and open to parody as its predecessor.

So maybe you look at your options and think, I don't want to write in Ye Olde Englisshe, but I also don't want it to sound like I've dropped the cast of *The Wire* into a fantasy world. Can I invent some slang?

Sure!

...good luck with that.

It *can* be done. And the people who pull it off well are *brilliant*. It's easy to forget, but the slang of *Buffy the Vampire Slayer* sounds realistic less because it imitated its period than because lots of people started talking like the show. The novel and film of *A Clockwork Orange* use Nadsat, a Russian-influenced argot that strongly contributes to the three-dimensionality of its invented future subculture. Russell Hoban took things even further with *Riddley Walker*, where the entire novel is written in an imaginary future dialect of English.

But most of us aren't going to go that far, and would face-plant if we tried. Instead we salt in a few terms here and there, as suits the story we're telling. Robin McKinley does such a good job with this in *Sunshine* that I curse myself for not thinking of it first; in that urban fantasy setting, much of the slang is mythological in origin, with the narrator saying she's "thor as hell" when she wants to describe her strength, or talking about charms "going kali" when they become unstable. "Spartan" is an all-purpose word in the vein of "cool" or "great." Even if your story isn't set in a variant on the real world, you can look for things in the religion or history or environment of the characters that might give rise to equivalent terms.

It's possible to fall down a rabbit-hole when you try to do this. If I recall correctly, Marissa Lingen has described this as the "moss-troll ichor" problem. You want to describe something as being the exact shade of green found in Nyquil, but there's no Nyquil in your world, so instead you say it's the green of moss-troll ichor—but your reader doesn't know what shade of green that is, and furthermore now you've added moss-trolls to your setting just for the sake of a description, and maybe you need to put some onstage so that the reader will understand what color their ichor is, and for crying out loud, all you wanted to do was say something was a very deep blue-tinged green color...which is why most writers will only put in a few touches of invented slang, where it will be the most useful.

Readers' mileage on this varies. Some find invented slang incredibly distracting, and would prefer you simply use "normal" English (for whatever value of "normal" applies to their speech community). Others will be kicked right out of a secondary-world fantasy if anyone says "okay," because to them that is too specifically modern. Some people feel you shouldn't use words like "galvanize" in a setting where there was never any Luigi Galvani, while others have no idea that's the etymology, or wouldn't care if they did. There's no pleasing everyone, and the more you try, the more bland and flavorless your prose is likely to become.

So by all means, stop and look at the metaphors your characters use to describe things, the touchstones they use for praise or condemnation, and ask whether changing those up can add depth to your world.

Folk Magic

In discussions of fantasy worldbuilding, you hear a lot of talk about magic *systems*. About how they need to have *rules*. And then you wind up with something like *Dungeons and Dragons* or Brandon Sanderson's various novels, where the magic is as codified and quantified as a video game.

This bears very little resemblance to magic in the real world.

By that I mean magic as people have believed in it for millennia, magic as it has fit into the structure of real societies. Of course, magic in fantasy novels often does things no real-world sorcerer has ever achieved, like hurling a fireball from their fingertips or turning a vampire into a lawn chair—and there's nothing wrong with telling stories about invented ideas of magic, any more than stories about invented aliens or other things that don't fit real experience. After all, we're talking about speculative fiction; speculation is the *point*.

But at the same time, there's a missed opportunity. Fantasy writers often get so caught up in the huge, overt, undeniable things that magic can do, they neglect to think about how it operates at the level of the common people—what an anthropologist would term "folk magic."

Folk magic is difficult to talk about because it isn't some kind of unified system whose underlying principles can be laid out in a paragraph or two. Folk magic is nailing a horseshoe above your door for protection (always open side up, so the luck doesn't drain out). Folk magic is eating black-eyed peas on

New Year's Day in the hope of bringing prosperity. Folk magic is trying to blow out every candle on your birthday cake in a single breath so that your wish will come true. It's superstitions and habits people don't even think about as superstition, because they're just what you *do*, and the suggestion that you should do otherwise would be met with confusion and disbelief.

The boundaries around it are so blurry as to be unidentifiable. The term is nearly synonymous with "folk religion," because a lot of it derives from religion or at least has overtones of same, and they share in common the general principle of lying outside official doctrine. Religion overall is a whole can of worms I'll have to spend multiple essays unpacking someday, but one thing stories often forget is that the orthodox form of a faith often bears little to no resemblance to how it's practiced by common people in the streets or the rural hinterlands. Educated clergy often cringe to see what hash the "ignorant" have made of their rituals; in the worst cases, folk magic becomes a sign of outright heresy and has to be obliterated before its poison can spread. In less extreme cases, it becomes regional variation, the sort of thing folklorists love to study. People mash together prayers, call on saints for off-label uses, build up folklore that connects some demigod to a particular hill and then people go to that hill because the stories say that if you bury three round stones at the hill's crest and then sleep there naked overnight during a full moon, you're guaranteed to get the spouse you want.

Does any of it *work?*

In a fantasy novel, the impulse is to say "yes." After all, aren't we reading and writing fantasy because we want to see magical things happen? But I'd argue that the "does it work" question has the wrong end of the stick to begin with. We're so accustomed to looking at magic from a modern, scientific, post-Enlightenment perspective that it's difficult to let go of the notion that an experiment must be replicable before it's significant.

The people in that hypothetical village are unlikely to assemble a blind study of hilltop rock burial and naked sleeping, to determine what the success rate is of the demigod granting people their marital wishes and whether this is affected by gossip in the village about the fact that someone is obviously angling for a particular husband because I heard she went to the hill last night. The point of that little ritual is to express intent—*I really want to marry this man*—and to create a sense of control. Whether or not the ritual works, at least you *tried*. You took action. Maybe your desired husband hears about what you did and is so touched that he proposes. Maybe doing the ritual gives you the confidence you need to catch his eye at the harvest fair next week. Maybe you're too shy and he doesn't like you and family politics mean the whole thing was doomed from the start, but when it all falls through you can reassure yourself with the memory that you did your best.

Folk magic is about belief. It's a net of delicate little threads that can rarely move the whole plot, but they connect people to each other, to the landscape they live in, to their religion and their history and their fears and their hopes for the future.

The presence of fireball-hurling wizards would not, I think, erase the need for that kind of thing in people's lives. If anything it might make the need stronger, as the common folk now have to fear not only the swords of the nobility and the judgment of harsh laws and the vagaries of the natural world, but the arcane powers of the magical elite. And on a narrative level, it adds a whole layer of texture to the story. A child is sick and her mother tries cures that have nothing to do with modern germ theory or pharmaceuticals; maybe it helps or maybe it doesn't, but either way it tells you a lot about the mother and the world she lives in, and it makes the mother seem more real.

Because when we face problems like that in real life, we cling to any belief that offers us hope and that sense of control. (Yes, even today.)

Lucky Charms

I don't have actual scholarly statistics to back this up, but I wouldn't be surprised if good luck charms weren't one of the most common—maybe *the* most common—concepts in folk magic.

After all, they're alive and well today, even when many other types of folk magic have become far less widespread. Do you have a lucky pebble in your purse, a lucky tie you wear to all your job interviews? Even when we know these things have no actual power, we often still make use of them, tongue only partly in cheek.

It's pretty basic psychology: if a given object is associated in your mind with one or more occasions when good things happened to you, then it's reassuring to have it on hand when you want things to go well again. I have a five-yen coin in my purse that I found when scouring the ground in Okinawa for my lost wedding ring three years ago; five (and fifty) yen coins are supposed to be lucky because of the holes in them, just as stones with holes in them are often reputed to be special, and hey, I found my ring not long after that. Maybe the charm's only effect is to soothe your anxieties a little bit when you're going into a stressful situation…but that's still a useful effect, and may cause things to turn out better as a result.

Pretty much anything can be a good luck charm. Some of them are codified; crosses, saints' medallions, holy relics, and other such religious objects often have that association in addition to their religious function. In the Middle East and North Africa, the hamsa or Hand of Fatima, a hand-shaped symbol, is a defense against the misfortune brought by the evil eye; the nazar serves a similar purpose through a similar geographic region. Male Roman children were given a bulla, female children a lunula—two kinds of protective amulets, needed because children are often seen as being especially vulnerable to malicious forces. In East Asia, the creatures variously known as shisa (Okinawa), komainu (Japan), or shi (China) are protective symbols, warding off evil spirits from important locations like temples. At Japanese temples you can also buy omamori, small amulets that bring good fortune, often for specific purposes like upcoming exams or travel safety.

But as my coin example shows, it can merely be a random item you associate with good luck, because it's pretty or something good happened to you in a related context or just, I dunno, everybody agrees that's how they work. Stones seem to be common for this, as are coins—especially, as mentioned above, if they have holes in them—but not all good luck charms are durable; four-leaf clovers are perishable but very well-known. Rabbit's feet are one of those things I took for granted until I stopped to think about it, at which point it started to seem a little gruesome. (I'm pretty sure most of the rabbit's feet you see sold in gas stations and the like are not made from real animal parts, though.) Horseshoes, mentioned in my previous essay, may derive some of their reputation from the iron they're made of, which in the British Isles was reputed to ward off faeries and their mischief—not to mention that blacksmiths have often been seen as having magical power.

Good luck charms are also behavioral. Have you ever knocked on or touched wood after speaking of your good fortune or the possibility of bad luck? The idea is that you're calling on the spirit of the tree to make sure malicious forces don't notice what you just said and decide to screw you over. Crossing oneself, spitting, turning around three times—there are all kinds of ritualized behaviors people may call on, whether they're codified in the culture or personal superstitions. (Taken too far, some of those things become manifestations of obsessive-compulsive disorder.) Blessings are a major category here, with various prayers and invocations asking the gods or their intermediaries to gift the target with good fortune.

My common refrain in these essays is, "I don't see this very often in fiction." Occasionally there will be a passing reference to a character "making a sign to ward off the evil eye," but we rarely get a description of what that sign is—maybe because gestures often take more words to describe than they're really worth. But if you put the first usage of it in a context where taking that time to describe it won't disrupt the flow of the narrative, and if you give it a name (like we might say "the sign of the cross" or "the fig sign"), then you can use it repeatedly later in the story and your reader will have a better sense of what it means. You can mention children wearing or receiving or losing their protective amulets, or your protagonist reaching into their pocket to touch a well-worn bit of stone, or streetside kiosks selling good luck charms of all kinds. This kind of thing might be less common in science fiction, because so much of that genre takes for granted the idea that people in the future will be less superstitious than they are today…but of course that won't necessarily be the case. And in fantasy worlds, you'd expect to see this kind of thing all the time, especially when society at large knows that supernatural forces have very palpable power to affect the world around them.

Curse You!

If good-luck charms are one of the most common types of folk magic, I suspect curses are right up there with them.

This time I don't mean profanity (though there's a degree of overlap there). I mean actual malevolent attempts to cause someone harm by supernatural means. Sometimes people do this deliberately, out of a desire for power or revenge; other times it's a subconscious process, the metaphysical consequence of negative emotions like anger, jealousy, or fear. The latter shows up in the Japanese concept of an *ikiryō*, a "living ghost" that is the projection of a person's spirit, or in the (I think) Asante concept of witchcraft as a thing people can do without meaning to or realizing that it's happening.

The deliberate versions are easier to talk about because they are, for obvious reasons, more concrete. Many curses amount to codified ill-wishing, with a profoundly fuzzy boundary between religion and magic—here taking "magic" in the sense of "supernatural means not approved of by religious authorities." Imprecatory prayer is the act of petitioning gods, saints, demons, or other such powers to bring misfortune on your enemies. In Greco-Roman times these were often written on curse tablets. Some religions think that kind of thing is totally fine; some don't; and some just avoid commenting on the fact that praying for your own side to be victorious in battle amounts to wishing for the other side to die. (Mark Twain commented on it, though.) Is it not a curse if the negative consequences for someone else are an ancillary effect, rather than the focus of your prayer? Is there a meaningful difference between "please, God, lead my side to victory" and "please, God, lead my enemies to defeat?"

That's a topic for theologians and ethicists to debate. We've got more than enough genuine, unquestionable examples of curses to keep us busy.

Consider the poppet, aka the "voodoo doll" (which does not actually originate with that religion). Operating on the principles of sympathetic magic, which hold that an object which resembles or contains a piece of the target has a connection to that target, people all over the world have crafted little dolls and figures for supernatural use, both good and bad. Sticking pins in the doll is meant to cause illness; burning it or "drowning" it is meant to kill the target. In Tamora Pierce's *Song of the Lioness* quartet, a number of poppets are tied up in a veil as a magical effect to prevent them from "seeing clearly," i.e. realizing what the villain is up to.

Fear of what malign sympathetic magic might do has led people to take precautions with their hair clippings, fingernails, and so forth, burning or otherwise disposing of them lest they be employed in a poppet or other curse. Execration texts leverage names for the same connection, which is why certain magico-religious traditions of both the real and fictional variety have practices designed to protect people's names against such threats.

Other types of objects can inflict ill fortune. Maybe you craft some sort of "hex bag" and hide it in the target's house or under their bed, or bury it under their front step. Or you bury it along a road or path you know they'll travel, and when they cross over it, the curse will attach to them (as long as nobody else comes along first...). Subtle, hidden curses of that sort are intended to be more difficult to detect and counter.

On the other hand, sometimes lack of subtlety is the point: the Indigenous Australian bone-pointing practice is a very public delivery of a death curse. The Germanic "nithing pole" or *niðstang* involves cutting off the head of a horse and sticking it on the end of a rune-carved pole, facing toward your enemy's house—which amounts to a neon sign announcing you wish your target ill, at least if you put the pole anywhere visible. (And looking those up on Wikipedia, I am weirdly charmed to find that some Indigenous Australians performed the bone-pointing ritual against their prime minister in 2004, and Icelanders stuck cod heads on poles in 2016 to protest *their* prime minister. Anyone who thinks such things are confined to the past is wrong.)

Curses can also be set up such that certain actions will trigger them, as with the protective spells sometimes placed on Egyptian tombs by priests seeking to deter grave robbers. Stealing precious objects from religious sites is in general a route to misfortune, for obvious reasons: angering a deity is rarely a good idea. Book thieves have been threatened since the days of Ashurbanipal; medieval European scribes warned them of a variety of punishments, ranging from mortal measures (excommunication, execution) to divine intervention (damnation). Breaking an oath may leave the traitor accursed in one fashion or another, which is sometimes laid out explicitly in the oath itself. People may place curses with their dying breaths, or the simple fact of their death may lay the curse—especially if the victim was the killer's kin, such acts being deeply taboo in many cultures (cf. Cain, or the Greek notion of the Furies).

As with good-luck charms, there's a psychological effect in play. The nocebo response is real; it's the opposite of a placebo, making negative outcomes or side effects more common if you expect them. Knowing someone has cursed you may have all kinds of effects, ranging from depressing your immune system to making you more accident-prone to drawing your attention toward the bad things that happen to you, causing you to see a pattern in them where another person might see random chance. Performing a curse against someone reinforces your dislike or opposition, which may encourage you to take other actions against them, or rally other people to your side. So even in stories not built around the assumption that things like curses have metaphysical force, the idea may still show up, because it still carries very real social weight.

Divination

Prophecy is all over the place in fantasy, to the point where it's become enough of a cliché that a writer has to tread carefully in using it. The Chosen One who will save everybody from the evil threat, the return of an ancient foe when certain conditions are fulfilled, etc. etc....been there, done that, could make a t-shirt out of the book covers.

Weirdly, though, divination doesn't show up nearly as much. By that I mean not the giant, earth-shaking predictions of What Is to Come, but the smaller, day-to-day attempts to get some supernatural guidance. This is a worldwide phenomenon, from ancient times to the present moment, because uncertainty is a universal thing in life, and so is the desire to allay it by one means or another. We watch weather reports because we don't want to end up cold or wet; we read stock market predictions because we don't want to lose our investments. And if we believe that there's a way to get information from spiritual sources instead of statistical models, we'll try that, too.

These days the most common version of that is probably the newspaper or internet horoscope. (How many of us read those with interest, even if we don't believe?) Calculating a horoscope is a fairly complicated process, though, requiring knowledge of astronomy; if you're talking about a pre-modern society, relatively few people are going to have the specialized education necessary to do that work. Astrologers have historically been advisers to the rich and powerful, who can afford to hire skilled professionals. For everyone else it was more often about seeing general omens in comets, shooting stars, solar or lunar eclipses. (Almost all of which tended to be interpreted as signs of calamity, though occasionally they heralded important births.)

Today most of us think of astrology as idle diversion at most, but it used to be very serious business. In Tudor England, calculating the horoscope of the king or queen was a crime, because you might be trying to determine when and how they were going to die. In the urban fantasy manga *Tokyo Babylon*, two *onmyōji* (yin-yang magicians) conceal the times and places of their births from each other, as a form of supernatural security. *Onmyōdō*, which is the Japanese term for a practice that originated in China, made widespread use of astrology in general to calculate auspicious and inauspicious days and directions; one day might be favorable for war, while on another day court nobles would avoid any business that required them to travel south, because that direction was temporarily ill-omened. Celestial bodies are sufficiently awe-inspiring, and sufficiently associated with the gods and other powerful spiritual forces, that it made sense to assume their movements and alterations were a message to or an influence on the earth below.

You'll sometimes see tarot in fiction, usually urban fantasy, where the writer leverages it to create foreshadowing or move an investigation forward by providing insight to the protagonist. Tarot-as-divination (contrasted with tarot-as-game) is a more recent phenomenon than many people assume, but in a secondary world you can make it as old as you like. Or invent your own version: the *Pathfinder* roleplaying game has a surprisingly good deck called the harrow, with an interpretive system that isn't just the tarot with a paint job slapped on top. But decks of cards as a widespread thing, whether for divination or play, pretty much require your society to have at least woodblock printing technology; if they're being made entirely by hand, they'll be quite expensive and rare.

When runes or bones show up in fiction, they're often much more handwavy, with some old crone tossing them onto the ground and then declaring whatever the plot needs. I suspect this is largely because readers and writers alike are less familiar with those methods, so there's less expectation that you'll show your metaphysical math. And while there's a relatively codified system for runic interpretation, at least as it's performed nowadays, the more generic "bones" are far less defined. We know that in Shang Dynasty China they used turtle plastrons and ox scapulae for divination, by interpreting the cracks created when a hot rod touched the material—but the principles behind that interpretation? Those are lost to time, at least until some archaeologist digs up an ancient Scapulomancy 101 text. Much more well-known is the I Ching, which can be cast with coins or yarrow sticks (though how the latter used to be done is again unclear).

Some kinds of divination are the realm of governmental officials and other formal figures, like the haruspices of ancient Rome or the onmyōji of Japan. In the highlands of Guatemala, the Mayan tzolk'in calendar is still used by daykeepers who must undergo a lengthy initiation; I was fortunate enough to take a class once from Dennis Tedlock, who along with his wife Barbara has been initiated as a daykeeper as part of his anthropological research.

But other forms of divination are very much folk magic, accessible without a long period of training or official certification. Bibliomancy can be employed by any literate person with a book in their house (in Christian Europe, usually the Bible). The behavior of animals or appearance of unusual cloud formations are there for anyone to see, and over time you'll get a handful of set interpretations, like the Japanese belief that a butterfly entering the guest room of a house means a loved one is coming to visit. In colonial New England girls would toss apple peels over their shoulders, which were supposed to land in the shape of the initial of the man they were to marry. Virtually any phenomenon, from the clumping of tea leaves to the barking of dogs, can be interpreted for information on the past, present, or future.

I don't expect that to go away any time soon. Science fictional futures where everybody is one hundred percent rational and never expresses superstition or religious belief are more difficult for me to believe in than faster-than-light travel. And in fantasy, you'd expect that kind of thing to be everywhere—but even there, divination rarely plays a role in the story. As authors, we reach for prophecy when we need it to steer the plot, but we forget to think about the aunt who pulls out her copy of scripture any time she has to make a decision, the queen who scrupulously observes directional taboos, the military commander who ignores the sacred chickens and regrets it at the Battle of Drepana. This kind of thing used to be pervasive, shaping many small decisions instead of just the big ones, and a story that remembers that will feel a lot more three-dimensional.

Birthdays

The New Worlds Patreon started up on the first Friday of March in 2017, so the first Friday of September was as good a week as any to declare the six-month anniversary of the series—and, in a happy coincidence, it was also my birthday, which gave me my topic for that week.

Birthdays seem like a simple idea, right? Celebrating the day you're a year older. Except it turns out there's way more variation in that concept than you might expect.

Let's start with the date itself. Here in the United States, most of us celebrate our birthday on the day we were born. But imagine you live in a preliterate society, or one where reading and writing, much less the tracking of calendrical dates, are the realm of educated specialists only. In that situation, you're unlikely to know the precise date of your birth, because "precise dates" aren't really a concept you deal with much at all. You'll calculate it in more relative terms: I might say I was born at the waning half moon before the fall equinox. (This is still how we calculate the date of Easter, which falls on the first Sunday after the first full moon after the spring equinox). Or I might not even remember that much specificity, and simply peg my birthday as happening in late summer.

That uncertainty probably contributed to the practice of celebrating a name day instead of a birthday. Though I think it's less common now, in Christian countries where people are customarily named after saints, you might celebrate on the feast day of that saint instead. *Those* dates will be known, because they're part of the religious calendar and have associated rites and traditions. In essence, this piggybacks off the work done by the aforementioned educated specialists.

But not every part of the world is concerned with having an individualized day for celebration. In the traditional system used by China and many countries within their cultural sphere, everybody has the exact same "birthday"—or rather, gets one year older on the same day, New Year's. Someone born a week before the end of the year will, in that reckoning, be considered a year older than someone born just two weeks later, a week into the new year. Which seems imprecise, when you're used to the individualized approach, but it makes a lot of sense in societies that emphasize the communal over the individual, and it saves a lot of mental arithmetic (my brother is more or less three years older than I am, but our birthdays are three months apart, so for a quarter of the year he's technically four years older).

Even calculating how many years old you are isn't standardized. The East Asian system has another quirk, which is that you're considered to be one year old when you're born – giving you credit for the time spent gestating, basically. But going back to that hypothetical baby born a week before the New Year: under that system, eight days after birth they're two years old. I'll admit my knee-jerk reaction is to think "wow, that's inaccurate"—but that's when you have to stop and realize that accuracy depends on what exactly you want to be precise *about*. Prioritizing the precise number of solar years since your date of birth is only one way to do it, and there's no reason that has to be the most important thing to track.

Regardless of when they fall, some birthdays are more important than others. I'll talk more about adulthood later in this volume, but for now I'll say that whatever birthday marks official adulthood in your society tends to be an important one; to pick one example, Jews traditionally become adults at age 13 for boys and 12 for girls, when they become *bar mitzvah* and *bat mitzvah* respectively (meaning son or daughter of commandment).

But formal adulthood isn't the only reason to mark an age out as special. In the United States, for example, 21 tends to be an important number for many people, because that's when they're finally permitted by law to drink alcohol. In Japan, there's a festival for girls who are three or seven years old and boys who are five, and (for reasons related to how they're written) the 77th, 88th, and 99th birthdays are also seen as noteworthy. In many parts of East Asia, including Japan, the 60th birthday is significant, because then a person has completed a full sexagenary cycle of the Chinese calendar. Sarah Monette incorporated an idea like this into her Doctrine of Labyrinths series; the society there uses two different counting systems, decimal and septenary, and under the latter, being 49 years old (7 x 7) is a landmark.

The final thing to note here is that sometimes cultures don't celebrate birthdays at all. Jehovah's Witnesses don't; Islam is divided on the matter, even down to the question of whether Muslims should celebrate the birthday of Muhammad. The early Christian writer Origen encouraged you to look upon your birthday with disgust. This seems to happen because of a desire for the group to differentiate itself from other religious communities (ones that *do* make a big deal out of the day), and/or because of the belief that birthdays are egotistical and draw your attention away from God. Whatever the reason, don't assume that everybody considers them a special occasion, worthy of commemoration.

Me? I celebrated my birthday to the hilt, with good food, the company of friends, and karaoke.

Childhood

Every culture in the world recognizes that there are some important differences between a newborn baby and an adult, a growing child and an elderly person. We all go through various stages of life, with the transitions between them sometimes marked by rites of passage (about which more in a later essay). But I initially typed "certain stages" in that previous sentence, and then changed it to "various"—because although the notion that we age is universal, the categories and what they mean are not.

Let's start this week with childhood, which seems like a relative no-brainer. You're a child until…okay, maybe not so much of a no-brainer. When does it end? In some cultures it's pegged to the physical changes that accompany puberty, as when we say that a girl who has gotten her first period "is now a woman." But of course we do not, at least in the modern United States, *actually* consider that girl to be a woman yet, not in any legal sense of the word.

In fact, childhood in many industrialized countries has become a hugely extended, amorphous thing, in part because of the amount of education now considered necessary or at least desirable before you enter the adult world of employment. You're generally required to be in school until your mid to late teens, and people in America without high school diplomas or their equivalent face a lot of hurdles. Jobs for which that high school diploma used to be sufficient now expect you to have a college degree. Even when college is over you may face grad school, medical school, law school, more and more school. You might not enter the "real world" until you're twenty-five. Or older.

Frankly, our concept of childhood or not-yet-adulthood is kind of weird and recent. Most cultures before the Industrial Revolution simply could not *afford* to let their young people fritter away two decades or more of life before they became productive members of society. If a psychologist sat you down for one of those word association tests, you might respond to "childhood" with words like "innocence," "play," and so forth. We think of those years as a time when we're supposed to be unencumbered, bounded about by rules but free to enjoy ourselves, to *find* ourselves. But try floating that notion to somebody from five hundred years ago and they're likely to look at you as if you've grown a second head: to them, childhood might more accurately be summarized as adulthood with training wheels.

That's not to say that people didn't love their children—they certainly did—but your years of joy and freedom and play, if you got any, might very well end by the age of six, if not sooner. Then you would be responsible for taking care of younger siblings, cooking meals, cleaning the house, looking after livestock, planting and weeding and harvesting, anything you were big and strong and sensible enough to manage. Quite a lot of things that many modern parents would be horrified to see young children doing—they're not old enough for that!

Except that what you're old enough for depends in large part on what the people around you expect and prepare you for. Japan has a long-running TV show called *Hajimete otsukai* (*My First Errand*), where they hand money to four- or five-year-old children and even some as young as *two* (the latter accompanied by that four- or five-year-old sibling) and send them off to the market to buy groceries. By themselves. In Japan, it's cute; in the U.S., somebody would call Child Protective Services.

And oh, those siblings? Bear in mind that without some form of reliable birth control (which will get its own essay in a future volume), you're going to have rather more of them than most of us are used to nowadays. The number varies widely from country to country, era to era, and lifestyle to lifestyle; mobile hunter-gatherers, for example, tend to have children roughly four years apart, because you need your first kid to be able to walk reasonable distances on their own before you have a second babe in arms, whereas for sedentary farming communities it's all hands on deck. (A feedback loop, in fact: the relative abundance of food in good years both allows for a larger population, and demands it to cover the labor of planting and harvesting.) But the TV show *Call the Midwife* is one of the only pieces of media I've ever seen that really tries to show you just how many children were underfoot and running around in the days before the pill. The overall population skewed *vastly* younger than we're used to nowadays, to a degree that is frankly difficult to imagine if you're not used to it.

As is the death toll. In early modern European cities, the infant mortality rate—children who died before the age of five—often hovered around fifty percent. That's *one out of every two children* who died young. Mostly of infectious disease, though malnutrition and accidents and so forth also took their toll; in these days of vaccination, the scourges of measles, mumps, rubella, whooping cough, polio, smallpox, and more have nearly been eradicated from our consciousness, rather than being the expected fate of half our children. (But not eradicated from our world, with the exception of smallpox. And some of the others are on the rise again, as vaccination rates decline.)

So what childhood looks like in your world will depend heavily on the associated circumstances. Your typical quasi-medieval fantasy setting without birth control or healing magic? Solo children or the 2.5 average of the United States will be outliers, while many families will have a pack of children running around and more buried in the ground. A wealthy, technologized society where disease has been eradicated and women control their own bodies? You might have to run ads encouraging your citizens to get with the baby-making, the way Singapore has done in recent years. And whether those children's lives are focused on work and responsibility or endless schoolroom learning or floating aimlessly around until they know what they want to do with themselves will vary every bit as widely.

Respect Your Elders

Just as every society recognizes that children are not the same as adults, I think every society, to one degree or another, has respect for its elders.

After all, age brings knowledge and experience, which are valuable things. When you're young, everything is new, and nearly overwhelming; the first joke you hear is the FUNNIEST THING EVER, while your first broken heart means YOU'LL NEVER BE HAPPY AGAIN. As your experiences grow, you gain perspective, and can maintain your equilibrium in the face of things both good and bad. Your toolkit for problem-solving expands, and you know which solutions are more or less likely to work. Small wonder, then, that elders tend to be leaders—at least in the absence of something like strict primogeniture that can transfer a title to a babe in arms. But the force of age reasserts itself even there, with the practice of regency, an adult ruling in the child's place until the child reaches their majority. (And sometimes past that point, too.)

"Respect for elders" is considered a hallmark of East and Southeast Asian societies in particular, because it's a major feature of Confucian philosophy. It's noteworthy that Japanese, unlike English, makes a distinction between the words for older siblings and younger ones; the former are *ani* (brother) or *ane* (sister), while the latter are *otōto* (brother) and *imōto* (sister). Birth order matters enough to be tracked on the vocabulary level.

Nor, despite the phrase "filial piety," does this apply only within a family: the higher-ranked and more senior students at my karate dojo are *senpai*, a term of respect whose etymology reflects the fact that they have gone before (it's the same *sen* as in *sensei*). The converse of *senpai* is *kōhai* (in Korean, *seonbae* and *hubae*). In its strict form the dynamic between those two can be quite hierarchical, with the junior using honorific language for the senior and performing all kinds of menial tasks, such as maintaining their *senpai*'s sports gear or cleaning the office.

But lest we think this is just an Asian thing, consider the English tradition known as fagging. It bears a very strong resemblance to the *senpai/kōhai* arrangement, though it's more limited in its scope (being confined to school rather than extending through work, hobbies, and other parts of society). Military organizations may have a similar dynamic, with new recruits being put through a hazing period of servitude before being accepted as real members of the unit. Such systems tend to be self-perpetuating: after you've been on the serving end of that dynamic, you often feel it's only natural or fair to enjoy your time on the receiving end.

The interface between seniority and age can be complicated. During a recent karate seminar in Okinawa, my husband and I got into a discussion of this with some of the younger black belts, on the topic of who is expected to pour drinks (water, tea, sake) for whom at dinner. In the karate context, the standard answer is that the lowest-ranking belt present should be pouring (*senpai/kōhai* at work). But my husband is forty, while the black belts in that conversation were in their early to mid-twenties. They unanimously agreed that they would feel wrong having him pour for them, even though he's a brown belt; in the calculus of seniority, the age gap is big enough to take precedence over the rank gap. Conversely, European aristocratic hierarchy sometimes had elderly noblemen bending the knee to sovereigns barely old enough to wipe their own noses. The relative weights of these things vary.

How old is old enough to be an elder? It depends on the society. Where life expectancy is low, forty might be enough to qualify you as a greybeard. Where people live longer, though, you might be sixty and fuming that you still haven't earned that level of respect. There might be a specific age at which you receive that distinction—perhaps a numerologically significant number—or it might happen when you reach a certain stage in life, whether that's social (retirement from your previous responsibilities) or physiological (post-menopausal women).

As for what happens when you achieve that status, again, it will depend on the society. Maybe you're no longer expected to engage in normal labor, but can sit back and let other people take care of you, earning your keep by dispensing your hard-earned wisdom. Maybe you can engage in special religious rituals, entering into mysteries the younger generations are not allowed to see. Although it's rarely defined on a formal level, elders can often get away with behavior that would never be tolerated from someone half their age; in particular, widows in the West have frequently enjoyed a degree of social and economic freedom that married women could never aspire to.

In theory, the rights and privileges that go with being an elder are counterbalanced by some degree of responsibility. Much like the liege lord in a feudal relationship of vassalage, a person with respected senior status is supposed to provide some benefit to the people below them: advice, instruction, patronage, protection, etc.

But of course, as with any hierarchical relationship, you'll have people who abuse their higher position to reap all the reward without giving anything in return. They may feel it's their right; as I mentioned above, after you've been through the grinder of the lower status, you may believe you've earned every bit of payoff you can wring from the situation. Or maybe the elder just isn't very qualified for the status they enjoy: while knowledge and experience *can* accumulate with age, it's also possible to make it through decades of life without gaining an ounce of real wisdom. Then the younger set find themselves in the awkward position of trying to figure out how to navigate around the elder's dumb ideas or unreasonable demands, without too openly flouting the customs of their society.

The United States these days tends to idolize youth to a remarkable degree. The Hot New Thing attracts attention, while the older employee/performer/etc. fades into the background, taken for granted at best, discarded at worst. We advertise a thousand products and services designed to make you look younger, because wrinkles and grey hairs, once badges of pride, now get treated as unsightly blemishes. But respect for age is more common than its converse, and we shouldn't lose sight of the reasons why.

Rites of Passage

You start out a child, you wind up an elder; in between, there are rites of passage.

These are the ceremonies that mark a transition from one social status to another. The iconic example is the transformation of a child to an adult, as seen in the Jewish *bar mitzvah* and *bat mitzvah*, or the Latin American *fiesta de quinceañera*. That particular threshold has more or less fallen by the wayside in modern white Protestant American society, but that doesn't mean we entirely lack rites of passage; graduation is one, and a wedding is another.

Something like getting your driver's license or the right to vote, however, is not—at least not according to the definition anthropologists use (laid out by a guy named Arnold van Gennep). A rite of passage, at its core, consists of three stages: separation, liminality, and incorporation. The first divides the individual from the social status they used to have; you *were* X, but now you are not-X. That puts you in a liminal zone, a term that indicates you are standing on a metaphorical threshold, neither fish nor fowl, ready to transform. Finally, incorporation removes you from your liminal state and makes you a member of the new group.

How is separation achieved? In a relatively stripped-down version like high school or college graduation, clothing is a major component. See somebody in a cap and gown? You know exactly what's going on. Same thing with a woman in a white wedding dress. Other ceremonies, especially in other parts of the world, may incorporate other elements, ranging from body paint to an all-night vigil to the use of hallucinogens to induce an altered state of mind. The passage to adulthood in a hunter-gatherer society can be a multi-day affair, with tests of skill or religious ceremonies not permitted to be seen by people of the opposite sex. Basically, the more obviously an individual is marked out and divided from the normal world around them, the easier it is to tell that you're looking at a rite of passage.

I have to say that, as a writer, the part after you've been separated out is the bit that makes me sit up and take notice. Folklorically speaking, liminal things are powerful, and they are dangerous. Societies depend on organization for their stability, and so anything that slips free of the usual categories is at a minimum charged with psychological power. Past the minimum? Being liminal is literally magic. For example, women undergoing Shinto weddings wear a white hood over their hair to conceal the demon horns they supposedly grow. And if you're writing fantasy…yeah. You can run with that "liminality is magic" idea as far as you like. Especially if the person undergoing the rite of passage gets separated from society, but never reincorporated (e.g. because something interrupts the ceremony).

But it would be a pity if they never got reincorporated, because that's where the parties happen! There are probably rites of passage that don't involve a big feast afterward, but it's such a standard element of reincorporation that I tend to take it as a given. More ceremonial stuff can happen, too, like the individual being formally welcomed by their new peers, or given their first chance to exercise the rights they've just gained.

Reincorporation especially matters if the separation and liminal stages were traumatic. Our modern rites of passage are usually pretty tame, but anthropologists have documented some pretty severe practices, with the person undergoing trials for which the word "torture" wouldn't be exaggeration. Is this done out of cruelty? No—at least not in general, though it's always possible that the individual in charge of the whole show is vicious and abusing their power. Rather, the idea is that the more you go through as a part of your rite of passage, the stronger a bond you feel to your new group when you join them.

I can attest to this, at least on a minor level. In college, our marching band had what we called "freshman cuts," which was the point at which freshman who failed to measure up to a certain standard would (theoretically) be cut from the band. We all knew this wasn't true—they wanted as many warm bodies on the field as they could get—and the college had rules against hazing anyway, so the various activities around freshman cuts were one hundred percent optional, and everybody knew it. If you didn't want to go through with them, nobody would say boo.

Me? I was majoring in anthropology and folklore. Of *course* I went through it.

And I came out the other side with the story of what the "Brown punch" was like my year, a story that got shared with the band members both senior and junior to me, just as they shared their own tales. I'll spare you all the details, saying only that every component of the punch was perfectly potable or edible and utterly revolting when combined with all the other ingredients...and that drinking it, though in no way a "fun" experience, is one I don't regret in the least. Because it did what it was supposed to: it created a bond, a sense that I had gone through a trial that had made me kin to everyone else who had done the same thing.

And that brings us to the final point, which is that rites of passage are a two-edged sword. Colleges outlaw hazing rituals because they make people who don't go through them feel excluded, and there have been excesses that leave people traumatized or outright injured. But such rituals also promote bonding and group identity, which isn't necessarily a bad thing. And while having a rite of passage to mark the transition from one life state to another may result in you being thrust into a new role before you truly feel ready for it, it also makes it crystal clear what your role *is*. Do you have the rights, responsibilities, freedoms, and privileges of a child, or those of an adult? A single person, or a married one? A civilian, or a member of a military group? Muddying the waters between those things may cause difficulty, as you're left uncertain of where exactly you stand.

Lineage

Because of the various holidays in the U.S., December is a time of year when people's thoughts often turn to family. So I used that month to start unpacking what exactly "family" means in a cultural sense.

It's an incredibly complex topic. Anthropologists are stereotypically fascinated by kinship; figuring out who counts as related to whom, and what that relationship means, gives you a roadmap of a society. By no means the only one—there are other social structures that matter every bit as much—but I don't think there's any human culture that doesn't have some concept of kinship, pervading the entire group. Even those who are considered to be without family are, in part, defined by that absence.

Unpacking all of this is difficult, but we can start with the concept of "lineage."

A lineage is, at its core, a group of people who can trace their descent to a common ancestor. How far back is that ancestor? As near or far as you want it to be. Among white Protestants in the U.S., we often don't think much beyond a grandparent or a great-grandparent. In societies with a clan structure, by contrast, the common ancestor might be the mythical founder of your entire clan, buried so far in the remote past that no one can actually list every generation in between. A special case of this is a moiety, the term used when the entire society is divided into two large-scale descent groups.

What about that verb, "trace"? What do we mean by that? It doesn't just mean that you're related; it means you're related in the right fashion, the one that counts (however your society determines that). Thanks to humans reproducing sexually, the notion of lineal descent breaks down into two basic categories: patrilineal, aka agnatic (traced through the male ancestor), and matrilineal, aka enatic or uterine (traced through the female ancestor).

Patrilineal descent is probably the more familiar of the two for most of the people reading this essay, even though its more formal structures have broken down a fair bit in modern western society. Odds are good—though not guaranteed—that you share your last name with your father, who got it from his father, and so on up the father chain until you run out of documented genealogy. Family names are a way of marking patrilineage, because they get inherited from the male parent, and women traditionally change theirs when they get married.

Prior to laws that permitted women to hold their own property, names weren't the only thing that got inherited: a man's land and possessions were also expected to pass to his son, following the patriline on down. If a man didn't have a son, the property might go to his nephew, especially if that nephew was the son of his brother instead of his sister. Why? Because a married woman joins the patriline of her husband, so anything that passes to her son is leaving her birth lineage for a different one, instead of staying in the family.

We'll leave the topic of inheritance there for now, because it's a giant rabbit hole in its own right. Instead let's look at matrilineality, which a) rarely shows up in fiction and b) is often misunderstood.

Matrilineality (tracing descent through the female line) is *not* the same thing as matriarchy (rule by women), though I often see the two terms conflated in fiction. You can and do get wildly patriarchal societies that are also matrilineal. Women do not necessarily hold all the property (or even any of it) by dint of being the locus of kinship; what often happens is that property still belongs to a man, and his possessions are inherited, not by his son—who belongs to the matriline of his wife—but by his sister's sons, because they're the ones who share a common ancestor with him. The uncle/nephew relationship rises to great prominence in these societies, and enatic nephews (related through a sister) are considered more closely related than agnatic ones (related through a brother).

There's evidence to support the idea that matrilineality is the older concept of the two, though short of time travel we'll never know for sure. It tends to go hand-in-hand with social structures that allow female blood relatives to assist each other with childcare (though that crosses over into the question of residence patterns, which we'll talk about a little later), and since there's reason to think that kind of cooperation was vital to the development of the human species, it makes sense that it would be the more basic form of lineage.

These days matrilineality is less common than patrilineality, but it's found in a number of places around the world. In particular, it's characteristic of a broad swath of Central Africa, plus various Native American tribes, certain parts of Southeast Asia, and Oceania. It also seems to be associated with clan structures overall, i.e. broad lineage groups that go well beyond what we would consider to be the nuclear or extended family nowadays.

I should note that everything I've said so far has assumed unilineality—a setup where you belong to only one lineage, whether it's agnatic or uterine. It's also possible to be ambilineal, tracing your descent through both sides. In those cases you often get to choose which lineage to join, perhaps at your passage to adulthood. In practical terms, many of us think of ourselves in ambilineal terms: we consider both sets of grandparents to be equally ours, and our mother's siblings to be as closely related to us as our father's. If there's a gap between the two sides, it's more likely to be based on geography or personal feelings than a sense that one type of blood relation counts for more than the other.

In fiction, almost every story I read either assumes patrilineal descent, or doesn't pay any attention to the question at all. It would be interesting to see more matrilineal societies—though I will say from experience (in writing *The Tropic of*

Serpents) that it can be difficult to wrap your brain around that shape, when you're used to thinking in terms of patrilines!

And there's a lot of room to play with the concept of lineage beyond the bounds of how it has manifested in the real world. A society that doesn't police women's sexuality might be more likely to trace descent through the mother's line, because it's a lot easier to be certain whose uterus a kid popped out of than who put the sperm there in the first place. A culture that's built around non-binary gender might find some other way of defining which lineage group you belong to. There are so many possibilities, and our stories have barely scratched the surface.

Third Cousin Twice Removed

What kinds of relatives do you have?

This seems like a simple question. But that's because we take our words and concepts so much for granted that we don't even realize the extent to which they're a cultural construct. Yes, there's biology involved...but our understanding of and way of talking about that biology is shaped by society, by which relationships we consider to be important enough to provide them with their own special words and which ones we don't.

In modern Anglophone terms, you have a certain set of possibilities. Parents: mother and father. Siblings: brother and sister. Children: son and daughter. Parents' parents: grandmother and grandfather, and then add "great-" as many times as necessary to mark previous generations; ditto for children's children and so forth. Parents' siblings: aunt and uncle, again with "great-" or "grand-" if you need to go up a generation to a grandparent's sibling. Children of someone in the aunt/uncle corner of things: cousins.

We do get a little complicated where cousins are concerned, enough so that many people nowadays aren't clear on how those terms even work. The children of my aunts and uncles are my first cousins. The children of my great-aunts and great-uncles—my parents' first cousins—are my first cousins once removed, i.e. one *generation* removed. So are the children of my first cousins. The grandchildren of my first cousins are my first cousins twice removed, because now there's a gap of two generations between us. The children of my parents' first cousins, on the other hand—who belong to my generation—are my *second* cousins. My kids and their kids will be third cousins to each other.

Confused yet?

Not all languages bother with those kinds of distinctions. They may just lump everyone under the generic label of "cousin," i.e. someone related to me in a fashion not otherwise defined. We do that in daily discourse, too, and also leave out another factor: while most of our kinship terms are paired by gender—mother/father, brother/sister, aunt/uncle, and so forth—we have only the one bare "cousin," with no specific terms to differentiate girl-cousins from boy-cousins. In a language with gendered nouns, on the other hand, that might be inherent; in Spanish I have to specify whether my cousin is a *primo* (male) or *prima* (female).

Nor is that the only distinction we roll right over in English. We do not, for example, distinguish between an uncle by blood (related to one of my parents) and an uncle by marriage (wed to the sibling of one of my parents)—but Persian does. Nor do we distinguish between an uncle on the maternal side and one on the paternal, but again, other cultures do. We don't have a formal term to describe how my husband relates to my brother's wife—are they in-laws? Ish? (In my family we sometimes jokingly call this an "out-law" relationship.) Or what about in a polygamous household? Are your father's other wives or your mother's other husbands also your mothers and fathers, or do you use another term for them?

Or let's take siblings. English makes only one distinction there, on the basis of gender. In some East Asian languages, though, seniority also plays a role, so that you have different words for an older brother (*ani* in Japanese; *gēge* in Mandarin) and a younger one (*otōto*; *dìdi*), an older sister (*ane*; *jiějiě*) and a younger (*imōto*; *mèimèi*). Obviously it's possible to note the difference in English, as I've done here—but those aren't standard kinship terms, the kind of thing you might find listed in a dictionary. They're descriptive phrases, and read somewhat awkwardly if you have one character regularly address another as "Elder Sister."

Then you have what these days we call a blended family, where the basic structure gets complicated by changes along the way. When you share one but not both parents with someone else, we call that person your half-sibling. When you share no blood relationship at all, but one of your parents has wed one of theirs, that person becomes your step-sibling, and the new spouse becomes your step-parent. Sometimes this gets extended to step-grandparents, step-uncles, and so forth. (Interestingly, though you might think the "step-" prefix indicates a degree of separation, in fact it seems to derive from an Old English word for "orphan.")

One of the reasons kinship categorization matters so much is that it defines the boundaries of taboo and permissible behavior. "Consanguinity" is the term for how closely you're related so someone, and in most places and times anything within the second degree—i.e. parents or grandparents, children or grandchildren, or siblings—is considered incest. Nowadays we also tend to think of first cousins as being too closely related, but that's a relatively recent development; it used to be quite common in the West, and is still common in other parts of the world, for a first cousin to be considered an ideal match. But consanguinity is one of the grounds on which a Catholic marriage can be annulled; if you're too closely related, your marriage is not merely ended (à la divorce), but was never valid in the first place.

It isn't always defined along purely genetic lines, though. As I noted in the previous essay, you may not be considered as closely related to your relatives on the matrilineal side if your society is patrilineal. For example, in East African Habesha Christianity, you can't be connected to your spouse within seven generations on your father's side, but on your mother's, the limit is four. Whereas in societies where clans or other large lineage groups are exogamous (marrying out), anybody who belongs to that group is considered taboo for you to wed, regardless of how much (or how little) genetic material you actually share.

In spec fic, of course, there's endless room to play with this. A society that has shed a lot of gendered trappings might speak only of parents, siblings, children, without bifurcating those into pairs of terms; Rich Burlew has done this with elven society in his webcomic *The Order of the Stick*. For a society where the nuances of familial relationship govern huge swaths of society, you might resurrect archaic phrasing like "sister-son" and "brother-son" to distinguish between two different kinds of nephew. Or you could invent kinship terms to get around the English-language clunkiness of constantly referring to characters as "Elder Brother" and "Younger Sister"—though if you're going to do that, you need to use those terms early and often so the reader will internalize them properly. And even then, some people will bounce off that as an added hurdle.

But maybe not as many as in the past. As our society becomes more multicultural, we become more aware of these practices in other communities. I watched the Chinese drama *Nirvana in Fire* around the time that the younger of my half-Taiwanese nephews became verbal enough to call his older brother *gēge*, a term I'd learned from the show; it's now entered my vocabulary and my consciousness in a way it hadn't before. Even if you use a different word, your East Asian readers may feel a thrill of recognition rather than confusion when they read about your characters making such distinctions.

Fictive Kinship

Fictive kinship is exactly what it sounds like: fictional kinship. Not the kind you find in novels (well, you *may* find it in a novel), but rather the kind that has no genetic component: it is, after a fashion, "made up."

But it would be wrong to consider these relationships anything less than real. Fictive kinship can be profoundly important on an individual or a societal level. Anybody who's ever seen the term "family of choice" floating around fandom knows that blood isn't the only thing that can make a relationship narratively powerful; many of you have probably experienced it in real life, too. But fictive kinship isn't simply a matter of being emotionally close to someone. It's a formalized connection that's recognized by the rest of your society.

There's a sense in which you could call marriage the most common and accepted form of fictive kinship. After all, it creates a new relationship out of thin air, usually (at least these days) with no meaningful degree of blood relationship at all; doesn't that count? As anthropologists use the term, though, fictive kinship lacks both consanguinity and affinity (i.e. marital connection). It's basically the "miscellaneous" drawer for relationships that are thought of in familial terms, but aren't those *other* kinds of family.

With marriage laid aside, the most widespread and familiar form of fictive kinship is adoption or fosterage. It creates a legal (or at least formalized) parent/child relationship where none existed before. The reasons for this can be manifold: nowadays the most common ones are either that the parents died, or that they're unable or unfit to care for their children.

But adults can be adopted, too. Japanese history offers many examples of families without sons—or with unsuitable sons—adopting someone else to be their heir; sometimes this was a cousin from some more distant branch of the family, but in other cases the adoptee was simply an agreeable young man. If the family had an available daughter, he might marry her as part of the adoption process, becoming a son-in-law and then a son. The lack of a blood relationship didn't matter nearly as much in that society as it tended to in Europe, where laws might mandate that only the issue of your body could be counted as your heir.

Fosterage is a slightly different affair. It still creates a type of parent/child relationship, but without transferring legal connection away from the birth parents. The historical model is different from modern foster care; instead of being an alternative to structures like orphanages or an on-ramp to (ideally) formal adoption, it was a way of building social bonds between families.

This might go in a number of directions. In the Celtic regions of the British Isles and in Iceland, higher-ranking individuals fostered their children to the households of their underlings. In other cases, a favored underling might be given the chance to send one of their children for fostering in the household of their superior, giving that child a leg up for future social advancement. Or it might happen between equals, particularly with an eye toward future marriage alliances. Or it might be a form of hostage-taking, raising an enemy's child in your own household as collateral for their good behavior, and indoctrinating them to your own ways in the process.

By contrast, marriage alliances have often been prohibited between people related by milk instead of blood. Prior to the invention of modern baby formula, a number of women were employed as wet nurses, i.e. responsible for breast-feeding other women's children. This could happen because ill health (physical or mental) or insufficient production meant the birth mother couldn't adequately feed her own baby, but it also happened a fair bit among elite women. Some of them didn't want to spend their time nursing; others were pressured away from doing so because nursing reduces fertility, and therefore means it will probably be longer before the woman gets pregnant again. (For elite men determined to get a male heir, that was a major concern.)

As with fosterage—of which this can be a type—milk kinship builds social bonds. Choosing a suitable wet nurse was quite an undertaking, because she was responsible not only for the health but often the rearing and education of the child; some people believed her moral character would be passed along in her milk. The lower-status families who fostered a child during the nursing years acquired a special connection to the higher-status family, because they became the fictive kin of that child.

This fiction sometimes carries every bit as much weight as a blood relationship. Islam prohibits sexual contact between a man and his wet nurse, and some branches extend that to all the immediate consanguineous kin of the wet nurse, so that (for example) a man cannot wed his wet-nurse's daughter, either. She is effectively his sister. "Milk siblings" are especially a thing when two children were nursing at the same time, one fostered, one the wet nurse's own child.

Then you have godparents, whose role varies widely depending on which community you're looking at. It's largely a Christian concept, though there are somewhat analogous things in other religions; they stand as formal witnesses during baptism, and afterward are considered to have a lasting responsibility toward the one baptized. The familial nature of that relationship particularly comes to the forefront when you realize that godparents are prohibited from marrying their godchildren, just as if they were related by blood.

Fictive kinship can go beyond these familiar categories. My parents never fostered my best friend, much less formally adopted her, but somewhere along the line they took to introducing her as their "other daughter," and I refer to her as my sister often enough that it was weird for me to type "my best friend" at the beginning of this sentence. In a different time or place she and I might have become "blood sisters" or "oath sisters," swearing a formal oath of connection and possibly engaging in a ritual commingling of blood.

Other kinds of mentorship beyond the spiritual responsibility of a godparent can acquire significance; the "cap parent" or *eboshi-oya* who bestowed the hat used in a Shinto coming-of-age ceremony could be very important, and the child might use one of the characters from the cap parent's name in their own adult name. Speculative fiction has even more room to invent new types of relationship that could fit into this category—what if your magic was somehow inherited from another, unrelated person, rather than through family lines? The possibilities are endless.

Residence Patterns

It's hard to talk about kinship without also talking about marriage, but I'm going to delay that for the time being, and spend a moment on the border between the two by talking about residence patterns: where people live, and with whom.

This topic was at the forefront of my mind when I wrote this essay because at the time I was in Massachusetts, visiting my husband's family for Christmas. We live in California, clear on the other side of the continent from them. My own parents live in Texas. This is relatively common in the twenty-first century United States, but in the grand scheme of things it's kind of weird. Historically speaking, and in many parts of the world today, people tend to live much closer to their family—one part of it or another.

The term for what my husband and I have done is *neolocal residence*. When we got married, we lived in Indiana (where I was attending grad school), nowhere near either his family or mine: in a new place, hence "neolocal." As with lineage, it usually skews toward either the male or the female. When a couple lives with or near the husband's side of the family, it's called *patrilocal* or *virilocal* residence; when it's the wife's side instead, that's *matrilocal* or *uxorilocal* residence. (The former term applies if it's the whole lineage you're staying near, the latter if it's only the immediate family.)

Who you live near isn't just a matter of chance or trivia. Staying near your own kin means that you remain an insider, and have your family around you as a source of support. Going to a new place means leaving behind your own networks, or at least putting them at a much greater remove, and becoming an outsider among strangers. It's no coincidence that the Chinese government has tried to encourage matrilocal residence; under the patrilocal model, daughters are "lost" to other households and towns, siphoning wealth from the family. As a result, China has an ongoing problem with female children being preferentially aborted, killed in infancy, or abandoned. Encouraging new households to form near the wife's family can theoretically help mitigate that issue.

There are all kinds of social structures around these residence patterns. In uxorilocal cases, sometimes the husband owes "bride service" to his in-laws, working for them (e.g. on a farm) in exchange for his wife. If inheritance is matrilineal, the couple may have what's called a "visiting marriage," where the husband and the wife live separately: she stays with her own kin and he stays with his, visiting his wife periodically, but mostly being involved with the upbringing of his sister's children. On the other hand, neolocal residence requires that the couple have enough resources to maintain their own household without assistance from kin, which often interrelates with things like average age of first marriage and the employment situation of both spouses.

Then there's the question of who's *in* the household. I said above that it's patrilocal or matrilocal if the society is organized such that whole lineages live in proximity to one another, but virilocal (literally, "man placed") or uxorilocal ("wife placed") if it's only the immediate kin. Which brings us to the topic of nuclear vs. extended families.

Most of us here in the U.S. live in nuclear family units, consisting of parents and their (usually immature) children. Sometimes it's a single-parent home, or sometimes there are step-parents or half-siblings involved, but the general principle of "two generations in one house" is what defines the nuclear family. Extended setups get more complicated: it may be a stem family (grandparents living with one of their children and that person's spouse, plus grandchildren) or more extended than that, with multiple adult children and their spouses and children remaining with the grandparents.

The power dynamics here can vary widely. Is the eldest male the patriarch, controlling the younger generations of the household? Or have the oldest generation moved in with their children because they need caregiving or financial support themselves? The former is more common when all the sons remain in the household, the latter with stem families or nuclear families that have expanded outward to accommodate the older generation. (That last is increasingly common in the U.S.) And I won't dive down the rabbit hole of domestic architecture today, but for now, take it as read that how you go about building your house has a lot to do with how many people are expected to live in it, and with what configuration of power.

Humans being what they are, of course, we don't always stick to these neat little boxes. Polyamorous families, whether informal or connected by law, extend the household in ways that aren't necessarily generational. Out here in the Bay Area, where housing prices are ludicrously high, I know an increasing number of people who have banded together with unrelated friends in order to afford a mortgage. In eighteenth- and nineteenth-century England and the U.S., the situation of two financially independent women living together was common enough that a term was coined for it: "Boston marriages". Some of those women were in sexual relationships with each other (and might have gotten formally married if they could have); others simply wished to live without being dependent on a man.

Or take college housing situations. I don't know if it's true, but I remember hearing when I was in college that by some old Massachusetts law, any structure housing more than six women and an unrelated man could be considered a brothel; by that definition, every single dorm on our campus was a brothel. Mixed-gender co-ops are similar. People may live together for all kinds of reasons, ranging from the financial ("it's the only way I can afford this") to the ideological ("I want to be in a community of vegans/queer people/Buddhists/etc.") to simple convenience.

Many speculative fiction novels, though by no means all, neglect the question of family. But unless your characters are all foundlings, they have or at least had parents, and quite possibly siblings or aunts or cousins, too. Those people are going to live *somewhere*. Taking a moment to consider where that might be will make the social network part of the story.

Marriage

I joked when I posted these next few essays, in February 2018, that the month of Valentine's Day was possibly the *wrong* time to talk about marriage…because for most of history, marriage has not been about love! At least not primarily, not officially, maybe even not ideally. The modern Western approach to the subject is, historically speaking, pretty weird.

Which is something people often lose sight of. The debates in U.S. politics over same-sex marriage have occasioned a lot of sweeping statements about "what marriage is" and "how it's always been," often from people with absolutely no sense of history—and often with an implicit assumption that a given approach can only be defended as worthy today if it has historical backing. But the truth is that many of us would not much like living under historical models of marriage, and if your goal is maximizing good in the world, looking to the past is not necessarily the best way to do that.

At its core, marriage is a form of alliance. These days it's first and foremost an alliance between the spouses, and usually for reasons of personal happiness, but that's a product of the general focus on individualism that dominates our society right now. It used to be an alliance between larger groups than that. Families, or lineages, or businesses, or estates, or even entire kingdoms: the people directly involved were representatives of those groups, rather than acting solely for themselves. This works because we are, at heart, social primates. Even if you're not personally fond of a relative, the fact that they *are* your relative tends to influence your thinking—especially once that relative has a kid, who is also a blood relation of yours. You're invested in that kid's future. And even if you're not, even if you shake off that sense of connection...the people around you probably haven't, and they're going to judge you if you hang your kin out to dry. There's a lot of social pressure saying that if your daughter or brother or mother or cousin has ties to another family, you need to respect that.

So when your family member weds someone else, you now have a stake in the joint venture that is their marriage, and you become allied with the other parties who have connected stakes. You may use the match as an opportunity to completely merge some of your assets, as when two companies come under one umbrella, or two countries form a single, larger one. Or you may just lean on that connection to get help when you need it: "Dear father-in-law, I'm going to war and could really use some troops. You don't want your daughter to be sad that I died on the battlefield, do you? Or your grandchildren to lose their father?"

Because kinship ties underpin this process, it isn't surprising that marriage has most frequently involved at least one fertile producer of sperm and one fertile producer of eggs. (Or hopefully fertile, anyway—sometimes that doesn't work out as expected.) The counterpart to alliance is inheritance; you often need or at least want offspring who will inherit the business, the land, the connections to the parent families. Adoption is also a possibility, but how much people treat adopted children as truly family vs. only technically family has varied a lot between cultures.

That doesn't mean marriage is always about reproduction, though. Women past the age of childbearing can and do wed; the same is true for people who are infertile for other reasons. Marriages can be celibate. Sometimes a society has conducted marriages where at least one of the spouses is below the age of puberty (though in those cases there's usually an assumption that reproduction will happen once everyone is capable of it). Conversely—and contrary to our stereotypes of the past—people don't necessarily get married as soon as they become fertile. In Elizabethan England, the average first age at marriage was somewhere in the mid-twenties, much like it is today…and for much the same reason, which is that people often weren't financially secure enough to set up their own households until that point. Getting married at thirteen was the province of the rich.

Moving to the sex-and-gender side of the equation: most genderqueer people in other parts of the world have historically not entered into formal matches—they might set up households, but without the ceremonies that link spouses—but there are exceptions; the Ojibwe *ikwekaazo* and *ininiikaazo* (who in modern English terms would I think be called transgender) appear to be among them. In the West African kingdom of Dahomey, men could be married to the sovereign, not as a sexual relationship, but as a form of politically-motivated kinship. I came across a reference from a historical English register about a wedding where the groom was noted to be "very slight and probably a woman," but the ceremony proceeded nonetheless. And nowadays, of course, same-sex marriage is increasingly common in several parts of the world.

"Who gets married" isn't just a question of age and sex, though. Social class and other such factors also figure into it. Some slave-owning cultures have permitted slaves to marry; others have not, or at the very least have not recognized slave marriages as valid. (This was common in the antebellum American South.) Or maybe marriage could happen, but only with permission; the ladies-in-waiting who attended upon Queen Elizabeth I couldn't wed without her leave, and got into massive trouble if they did it in secret. As I mentioned above when discussing age, if getting married requires a certain amount of money—we'll talk about dowries and bride prices and so forth later on—then anybody without that money can't get hitched, even if they otherwise fill the requirements.

All of these are real-world examples, but let's not forget that we're talking primarily about speculative fiction worldbuilding. The barriers to marriage, or conversely the situations where it might be desired or mandated, can be anything that fits your setting. Marriages can happen for purely ceremonial reasons, which opens up a whole slew of possibilities in fantasy especially; the *hieros gamos* or "sacred wedding" is a term mostly applied to symbolic or sexual rituals rather than ongoing partnerships between mortal humans, but the latter approach offers all kinds of storytelling potential. Or maybe your science-fictional aliens can only trigger their reproductive capacity (and therefore their eligibility for marriage) by killing and eating a certain kind of prey, and that prey has become scarce, or your story is about a particular alien who is an abysmal hunter with no hope of ever making that happen.

Of course, it's also possible to fall off the ledge of historical accuracy in the other direction, assuming that marriages in the past were *nothing* like they are today, rather than exactly the same. Just because people didn't generally get hitched for the primary purpose of love and personal fulfillment doesn't mean those things never happened. For every cruel father who forced his daughter into wedlock purely for profit, there was another who realized the alliance would be a lot more successful if the parties involved didn't hate each other. People did take personal compatibility into account, and the ideal was often for that to go hand-in-hand with larger considerations. It's just that, given a choice between a sensible alliance without romance and two lovebirds who would bring no benefit to anybody but themselves, the tendency was to choose the former—as it still is in various parts of the world today.

Structures of Marriage

Having discussed who can get married and what reasons they have for doing it, let's talk about what shape the marriage can take—by which I mean how many people are in it, and how they're officially connected to one another.

For most of us, monogamy is the most common structure (mono- meaning "one," and -gamy meaning "marriage"). That is to say, someone in a monogamous marriage has only one spouse. That person is most commonly of the opposite sex, but not always, especially these days. But unless you come from a religion or a culture that absolutely forbids remarriage after divorce or death, monogamy doesn't mean having only one spouse, period; it means having only one at a time.

This stands in contrast to polygamy, i.e. many (or rather, multiple) spouses at once. We have a tendency to treat this word as if it means "multiple wives," but it doesn't: in fact, there are two more specific words to differentiate multiple wives (polygyny—the second part meaning "woman") from multiple husbands (polyandry—"many men").

The confusion probably arises because of the two, polygyny is the much more common structure. There are lots of reasons for this, many of them related to the patriarchal nature of most societies; when men held power and women are treated as property, then it's not surprising that the most powerful men will accumulate a larger share of that property to themselves.

That doesn't mean polyandrous societies are matriarchal, though. You see that pattern mostly in the Himalayas, where it's a solution to the problem of inheritance and limited resources: dividing up the land between all your sons means pretty soon nobody will have enough to live on, so instead you marry all your sons to a single woman—fraternal polyandry. The land stays in one family, and there are fewer children, so you don't wind up straining your resources. (Other societies accomplish the same end by shipping spare sons off to monasteries instead.)

Polygamy is illegal in the United States and many other Western countries. We tend to have a negative view of it in this country, associating the practice with Mormon fundamentalists in the Mountain West, living isolated from the outside world and engaging in abusive practices including, but not limited to, marrying adolescent girls to older men. It's also found in some Muslim-majority countries, and used to be legal for Hindus in India until the mid-twentieth century, not to mention historical practices in Judaism—in fact, if you look at history, there are many parts of the world where it was once common.

Is polygynous marriage bad for women? That's a difficult question to answer. It *can* be—but then again, so can monogamous marriage. Sometimes the senior wife is cruel and controlling toward the junior wives, but sometimes having co-wives is a source of comfort and support, especially when it comes to tasks like child-rearing. One of the sources I read when researching polyandry for *Within the Sanctuary of Wings* pointed out that being alone among a group of brothers can be incredibly isolating for women, contrasting that directly with the more female-dominated community of a polygynous marriage. In the end, it's tough to disentangle the actual effects of polygyny from the surrounding tendencies toward patriarchy, away from women's education, etc.

I do want to note, though, that what I've been discussing so far is polygamy in its more traditional sense, rather than the modern practice of polyamorous relationships (which in most cases can't be legally recognized as marriages). The former is very much a setup where multiple people of one sex are married to a single person of the opposite sex, without necessarily implying relationships directly between the same-sex partners; the latter is often (though not always) more communal and egalitarian, and is sometimes termed "group marriage" instead, especially if all or most of the spouses have sexual relations with each other. Line marriage, found in Heinlein's fiction, is a variant on this where the marriage itself becomes a kind of lineage, adding new partners over time so that the family unit eventually contains none of the original founding spouses. And then there is the sedoretu of Ursula K. Le Guin's fiction, where all marriages are expected to have two men and two women, with some internal relationships required and others forbidden.

There's also a separate-but-related subject in the form of concubinage and the keeping of official mistresses (or, more rarely, male lovers). That one is complex enough that I'll save it for an essay in a future volume, but I want to note here that its more formalized version amounts to a type of polygyny wherein the junior women occupy an inferior status relative to the senior ones, and its less formalized version amounts to a type of polygyny with no legal recognition for anyone other than the official wife. Both have tended to be the province of wealthy and powerful men.

Which brings me around to the social effects of these different structures. I mentioned in the previous esssay that one of the factors controlling who can get married is money; that's even more true when multiple spouses enter the picture, because now you need to support even more people. When each wife is expected to maintain her own separate household—one of the methods used to reduce intra-family strife and competition—the outlay is substantial. Men in polygynous societies may take second wives for reasons ranging from status to political alliance to the need for an heir when the first wife is sick or infertile...but in such cases, the lament that they're having trouble saving up enough money to afford that becomes very common.

And then consider supply and demand, so to speak. The human birthrate is basically 50/50 male/female. If some men are claiming multiple wives, that means other men have none. (Unless you have a society that is simultaneously polygynous and polyandrous. I don't think that's ever existed in reality, but now I want stories where it's true.) This can work if you have a warlike society and a decent number of your men are getting killed in battle, skewing the overall gender balance toward women—and there's a feedback loop there, because if you have a lot of young men running around without families of their own, the odds that they're going to enter into violent conflicts go up, unless you stow them somewhere safe like a monastery.

It's almost certainly going to be *young* men, too. Back when I talked about stages of life, I mentioned that power and influence (and money, though I didn't say it there) tend to accumulate in the hands of elders. Spouses go hand-in-hand with such things. Couple that with the risk of dying young in childbirth, which has been a serious danger for women throughout much of history, and you inevitably wind up with lots of situations where older men are marrying much younger women. It doesn't happen *only* because of patriarchal tendencies; it's also the natural consequence of other factors.

So if you want to write about marriage structures other than the type of monogamy that's common today, think about what factors will support that other structure, and what the effects of it are likely to be.

Buying and Selling Spouses

When marriage is more of an economic transaction between families than a union of two people for reasons of personal attachment, it isn't at all surprising that money gets involved.

There's good reason for this. Taking a new person into your household entails new expenses; conversely, the household losing that person loses the benefits of their labor. How that ledger gets balanced—who ends up being seen as needing compensation for the shift—varies depending on place and time.

The version most people have heard of is the dowry: wealth given by the bride's family to the groom or the groom's family as part of the marriage deal. It provides endless fodder for romance novelists writing historical tales, because much like college in the United States nowadays, it can be a big expense, and one families have to plan for early if they want to handle it right.

One of the ways to view a dowry's function is that it "purchases" a husband for the daughter, and as with anything else, the more money you have, the better a product you can buy. You can also cast dowry in modern terms as the startup fund for a household—especially when you consider the different forms it might take. Money is one possibility, but household goods like linens or furniture are another; assembling your trousseau was a very practical thing once upon a time (and still is in some places), and in such situations a girl who can show off excellent needlework skills is more attractive than one who can't sew to save her life. And then, of course, there's land: the dowry of a royal bride might include entire cities or provinces.

Dowry might also be a form of inheritance for the bride, and therefore of financial insurance—but how well that works out depends on the situation. If the bride retains control of her dowry, that's one thing, but if the groom or his family controls it, then it's all too easy for a feckless husband to fritter it all away. In theory a husband is often liable for returning the dowry to the bride's family if he sets her aside or their marriage is otherwise ended, but historical records are full of lawsuits over the failure to do so. (And also of husbands murdering their wives to avoid having to give up the dowry—not an accepted practice, but one that happens nonetheless.)

But that's only one approach to the marriage transaction. The inverse of dowry is bride price or bridewealth: the groom or his family transferring property or wealth to the bride's family. Sometimes this is again a form of financial security for the bride, but in other situations it's very much not, depending on whether her family is expected to return the bride price in the event of the marriage failing. It also theoretically demonstrates the husband's ability to support a wife.

Then there's dower—which, despite the similarity of sound, is not the same thing as dowry. It's more akin to bride price, in that it's a payment made by the groom, but in this case it goes directly to the bride herself, rather than to her family (though it may be held in trust in some fashion). This takes a bunch of different forms, and the legal intricacies are too much to get into here, but it's generally based on the idea that the wife depends on her husband for financial support, and if he dies or divorces her, she'll need something to keep her afloat.

You might think that pre-nuptial agreements are a modern thing, and the province of rich people who expect to have ugly divorces a few years down the road. In fact they're quite old and often quite necessary, even for people who don't have much in the way of property. As with any type of legal transaction, it's better for all involved if the terms of the deal are laid out unambiguously, and documented for future reference. In Judaism there is the ketubah; Islam also has marriage contracts. Other societies may have written documents specifying the dowry, bride price, dower, or other financial arrangements, especially in the event of one spouse's decease—at which point they intersect with the broader category of wills.

How these things fit into their respective societies is a complex question, and the details are a matter of debate among anthropologists. Are dowries more common in cultures where capital is the primary source of wealth, and bride prices in cultures where that honor goes to labor? Are one or both of these demeaning to women, or a beneficial way of providing for them and their future? What significance can you read into the form the gift takes, be it money or land or goods? What factors cause the expected gift to rise or fall in value?

It's a little easier to talk about the effects of such things. Being required to pay money up front before you can get married means that people without much—relative to their social class—are going to have a harder time getting married. (And don't think that shipping your spare daughters off to become nuns will solve the problem: some convents required a dowry, too, before they would take in a new novice.) This leads to people marrying later, or borrowing from their relatives to raise the necessary sum, or even engaging in crime—stealing cattle, for example, if you're expected to pay bride price in the form of a herd. In Europe, one of the pious and charitable things you could do was to fund dowries for girls with none. And the dower-style terms of a ketubah are in part a workaround for the problem of an up-front sum, letting a husband essentially promise money later, when he's more likely to have financial security, rather than having to deliver it at the outset.

Such things have mostly fallen by the wayside in the United States and other Western countries, but that doesn't mean they're entirely gone. Remember me saying that a bride's trousseau was material she brought into the marriage, for the setting up of a new household? Now think about wedding registries, which can fill the same practical function. And think about the custom, still widespread today, of the bride's family paying for the wedding and reception. There's expense associated with marriage—quite a lot of it, if you let the wedding-industrial complex talk you into all the optional bells and whistles—and we still have to answer the question of how to pay for it today. It's just the priorities and details that have changed.

Divorce

It's common for Christian wedding vows to include the phrase "till death do us part"…but the truth is that marriages don't always last.

The circumstances under which they can end, though, range all over the board. Who's allowed to call it quits the husband, the wife, their families, some higher (secular or spiritual) authority? What cause, if any, is required before you can cut the tie? What hoops do you have to jump through, and what are you allowed to do afterward?

At the most restrictive end of the spectrum, you have the Catholic prohibition against divorce. Annulment, which the Church permits, is not the same thing: that doesn't end a marriage, but rather declares that it was never valid in the first place. (Consanguinity, forced consent, killing one spouse so you can marry another, holy orders or vows of chastity, and various other factors can mandate an annulment.) At the most permissive end, for comparison, "triple *talaq*" allows a husband to divorce his wife just by saying "I repudiate you" three times.

One of the primary factors in the regulation of divorce is the protection of women. Many Muslim countries and schools of jurisprudence, going all the way back to the days of Muhammad, condemn triple *talaq* because it kicks the wife out into the cold with basically no warning or recourse at all. The Catholic prohibition is based on the idea that the bond created by marriage can't be dissolved by human action, but it also prevents husbands from abandoning their obligations to their families. The more a society makes women dependent on men for their financial support and protection, the more important it is to make sure they can't easily be set aside.

But of course requiring people to remain married can be detrimental in different ways. The same patriarchal structures that make it difficult for women to support themselves outside of wedlock tend to create power dynamics within the marriage that don't do those women a lot of good, either: an abusive husband can be worse than scraping to make ends meet on your own, and attempts to "reconcile" couples in such situations often amount to telling battered wives that things will be better if they just submit to their husband's authority. Formal separation can be a way around this; the two parties remain married in the eyes of religion and/or law, possibly with some financial obligations, but they no longer maintain a household together or remain married in the day-to-day, relationship sense.

Let's get back to those initial questions. Who can end the marriage? If a union has to be recognized by the church and/or state to count as valid, then those same institutions generally have to validate a divorce, too. But it's also sometimes possible for them to *initiate* the separation, even against the will of the husband and wife—especially if you want your fictional society to be a bit dystopian! Families have definitely exerted their political clout to break apart marriages, sometimes for the benefit of their kin trapped in a bad match, but sometimes for reasons of their own political benefit, like being able to then wed one of those people to someone else, or go to war against someone who used to be your ally.

More often, though, divorce is initiated by either the husband or the wife. As you can imagine, it's much more fair if they have equal right to do so—and I'll note that in the modern U.S. and U.K., where that's true, women file for divorce about twice as often as men do. (Why that might be the case is left as an exercise for the reader.) If only one spouse is permitted to end a marriage, it's usually the husband, which is why you get structures that try to limit how easily he can do so: he generally has less to lose in the process.

One way to limit ease of divorce is by only allowing it when sufficient cause can be shown. (If no cause is needed, it's called "no-fault divorce," which has been on the rise worldwide for the last fifty years or so.) The causes can usually be summarized as a failure to uphold marital vows or duties: adultery is a very common reason, but others include abandonment, cruelty (i.e. abuse), and so forth. Non-consummation—i.e. failure to have penis-in-vagina sex—usually results in annulment rather than divorce, because the marriage isn't valid until it's consummated, but failure to have children sometimes counts, whether that's caused by impotence, infertility, or just not living up to your marital obligations in bed. (This isn't necessarily gender-skewed the way you might expect: wives can and do bring complaints against their husbands for insufficient nookie, especially in polygynous marriages.)

Speaking of gender. .not living up to your gender role can be cause for divorce, and I don't just mean in the sense that you've committed adultery with someone of your own sex. If I recall correctly from my thesis reading, women in Viking Age Scandinavia could divorce their husbands for "effeminacy"— which included wearing clothing that was too girly. (Careful how many ruffles you put on that shirt, guys! The entirety of aristocratic Renaissance Europe would have been disqualified on the spot.)

Divorce can also be limited through mandatory waiting periods. These provide opportunities for reconciliation attempts—which may also be mandated—but also sometimes serve the practical purpose of making sure the wife isn't pregnant before the marriage gets dissolved. Charging fees for the process discourages people from quitting, and so does the thorny issue of who gets to keep what property and other resources after the split, which is a whole legal industry nowadays in the United States.

Finally, though, I want to note that sometimes a marriage isn't *intended* to last. There's some evidence that Scotland used to recognize handfasting as a form of limited-time marriage, though historians debate that; it's definitely true that a few schools of Islamic thought allow for such a thing, though most don't. (I discovered this through an article, which I have now sadly lost, that discussed how some modern jurists support it nowadays on the grounds that young people in cities are going to be having sex regardless, and it's better for them to do so within the bounds of at least a fixed-term marriage rather than outside it entirely.)

What about after divorce? If anybody gets the short end of the stick, it's usually the ex-wife, who may have no means of support and whose family may not welcome her back, especially if her dowry was forfeited in the divorce. She may be allowed to remarry, but might well face an uphill struggle in doing so; her ex-husband often has an easier time of it. But it depends heavily on how common divorce is in that society. If marriages regularly fall apart for one reason or another, then there's much less stigma associated with being divorced—especially if you can convince your next spouse that it wasn't any fault of yours. When it's rare and difficult, however, future prospects are more likely to give you the side-eye, if re-marriage is permitted at all.

Which means that people who want out of their marriage have to answer a hard question: which is worse? Sticking around, or dealing with the consequences of leaving?

Funerary Customs

Since October is, for many of us, strongly associated with Halloween, it seemed like an ideal time to talk about things related to death!

This set of essays began with funerary customs—which is to say, the question of what happens to the body of the deceased.

One option is to try to preserve the body as completely as possible. Mummification is most strongly associated with Egypt, but it's found in many other places as well—pretty much anywhere with an arid climate, whether hot or cold. (And then you also have bog bodies, which are essentially the inverse: waterlogged and acidic conditions dissolve the bones but preserve the soft tissue.) The earliest mummies were accidental, with the environment desiccating flesh before it could rot; then people saw that happening and started looking for ways to do it on purpose. Sometimes they mummified the whole body, while other times it was just the head, or another body part like a hand.

The modern iteration of this is embalming. Mostly that's a temporary measure, designed to keep the body from decaying unpleasantly during the funeral arrangements, but not always; the remains of Lenin are still on display in his mausoleum, as lifelike as modern chemistry can make them. As with ancient mummification, the truly elaborate treatments tend to be the domain of the rich and powerful, who can afford (or whose families can afford) the necessary materials and expertise. The average citizen rarely gets such expensive handling.

And then, moving toward the science fictional end of the spectrum, we have cryonics: low-temperature preservation done, not merely to prevent decay, but to theoretically enable later resuscitation. The effectiveness of that has yet to be established, but it's a common trope in novels—one with the potential to revolutionize a culture and how it relates to death.

Some societies go in the complete opposite direction, using cremation to destroy the body as thoroughly as possible. This practice is found worldwide and throughout history; in modern times it's strongly associated with Asia, due to the influence of Hinduism, Buddhism, and other major religions that advocate cremation. It's also gained a fair bit of currency in the modern West, as a much less wasteful alternative to burial (which can be quite expensive and creates problems for both land use and public health).

But some faiths disapprove strongly of cremation. The "religions of the book" generally forbid or at least discourage it, for reasons ranging from perceived disrespect for the dead to its possible interference with the eventual resurrection of the body. And according to a professor of mine, the Zapotec in Oaxaca dislike cremation because the period after death is supposed to be a gradual transition from a *nayaa* state (living, green, wet) to a *nabidxi* one (dead, brown, dry). Cremation short-circuits that process—kind of turning you into an Instant Ancestor.

Of course, cremation doesn't unmake the body entirely. It reduces it to ash, and in most cases there will also be some bone fragments left. What do you do with these? Scattering them to the wind is a common image, but so far as I'm aware, it's a relatively modern idea. More often the ashes would be placed in an urn or other container and then placed somewhere else, like a mausoleum, a place of pride in the house, buried, and so on. It depends a lot on how the living expect to interact with the dead.

This brings us around to burial, the other major funerary practice. Obviously you can (and sometimes do) bury a mummy or ashes, but at this point I'm talking about direct interment.

Archaeologists separate this practice into two types: primary burial and secondary burial. The latter describes situations where the remains are first placed in one location (the primary burial), and then later moved to a different one This is often connected with excarnation, the practice of defleshing a skeleton; you initially deposit the corpse in a place such as a cave or on a platform, then gather up the bones once the soft tissue is gone and shift them elsewhere. It's also considered secondary burial when, as happened in Europe, you had to relocate bones from a grave to make room for a new occupant, or whole cemeteries had to be uprooted and replanted elsewhere. (The catacombs of Paris are a famous example.)

How do people get buried? In any way you can imagine, and also in ways you probably haven't, unless you're an archaeologist. Directly in the ground, or with fabric wrapped around the body. On a bed. In a mausoleum. In a large clay pot. In a Cadillac—admittedly, that one's an unusual modern example. In a coffin or sarcophagus: prone, supine, curled on the side, standing, or head down (sometimes as a punishment). Sometimes the body is positioned so that the head points in a cosmologically significant direction. In Japan people avoid placing their beds with the head to the north, because that's how bodies are laid out before cremation; in Christian tradition, the dead are often buried with the head to the west, so that they will be looking in the direction of Christ's second coming.

Where do people get buried? Just about anywhere you can imagine ditto ditto. In the modern West we tend to assume that cemeteries are large swaths of land placed some distance away, but in the past churchyards were often local and small (hence the need to relocate bones). Important people got burials within the church itself, either in an above-ground tomb or the floor, with a paving slab to serve as a grave marker. In other parts of the world, the dead might be buried under the floor of an ordinary home. Crossroads burial, like head-down positioning, sometimes shows up as a punishment or way to trap a spirit. In ancient Rome the necropolis was customarily outside the city walls, while elsewhere it might be a greater distance away, either to keep the dead well separate from the living or because of geographical symbolism.

Sometimes graves are individual; sometimes they're shared by a whole family; sometimes they're mass burials, though when it's primary burial that's usually because of a battle, a plague, a massacre, or some other atrocity that discourages or renders impossible more individualized treatment. As usual, rich people get fancier burial locations—ornate tombs or pyramids or what have you—while the common folk don't.

Those are the most common ways to deal with the body of a deceased person, but not the only ones. Tibetan sky burial, for example, is an example of excarnation, but without actual burial afterward. And there's one significant custom I've skipped over here, because it will get its own essay in a moment—can you guess what it is? (No points for peeking at the table of contents.)

Cannibalism

Continuing the theme of death and its customs, I'd like to talk about the rather squicky topic of cannibalism. If that disturbs you, I recommend skipping the rest of this essay.

From a worldbuilding point of view, I think of cannibalism as a third rail. It's a custom that exists (or at least has existed) in reality, in many parts of the world, but including it in a story is difficult—at least if you want to use it for any purpose apart from Othering a society or showing how evil your bad guy is. Eating human beings is, for (probably) all of us reading this essay, so profoundly taboo that the simple horror of it can overpower anything else the author might be trying to say. Empathizing with it as a cultural practice? That's right out.

But that's why I decided it deserved its own essay. Because there's more going on here than you might assume, and while I don't expect to see it showing up in fiction a lot any time soon—nor should it, necessarily—it's worth giving the idea a proper look.

First let's talk briefly about cannibalism *not* as a cultural practice. By this I mean two things: first, when it's done for survival, and second, when it's done by a mentally ill person (e.g. a serial killer). Survival cannibalism is your Donner Party type scenario, where people stranded under starvation conditions resort to eating the dead from sheer desperation. This has happened countless times in countless places, but I'm discounting it simply because it isn't a part of the culture. (Though cultural responses to it can be interesting: are the people forgiven on the grounds that they had no other choice, or shunned for their taboo behavior?) The same goes for the serial killer situation, where it's an individual aberration from the norm.

With those laid aside, you can sort the cultural practice manifestations into two forms: endocannibalism (eating members of your own social group) and exocannibalism (eating outsiders). These may involve the same general act, but the meaning attached to it and the motivation for doing it are often very different.

Exocannibalism is what we tend to think of when the term "cannibalism" comes up. It's aggressive, dominating, an expression of superiority of the consumer over the consumed or an attempt to take the power of the consumed into oneself. Was your opponent brave in battle? Then perhaps eating his heart or other flesh would allow you to absorb his courage, making yourself even stronger for the battles to come. (A similar symbolic logic sometimes attaches to eating the flesh of certain animals.) In other cultures, your enemy's defeat in battle means he was weak and pathetic, and by eating his corpse you assert your final victory over him. When you read colonial-era accounts of "cannibal islands" and other such lurid tales, they're often talking about exocannibalism—when they're not making up slanders for the sake of justifying imperial conquest or extermination.

Endocannibalism is generally very different. It's a mortuary practice: something done for members of your own community to help them pass on from this life, by freeing them from their body, by taking their spirit into yourself or your community. Rather than being hostile, it's compassionate. Depending on the society, it might be expected that people will consume their own close relatives, that they will consume more distant relatives, or that the dead should be consumed by people as unrelated to them as possible.

This is *not* simply an unusual culinary practice. I learned a great deal about endocannibalism when one of my grad school classes assigned me to read *Consuming Grief* by Beth A. Conklin, which discusses the practice among the Wari' Indians of the western Amazon, and one of the things that stayed with me was the lengths they went to in order to ensure that the remains of the dead were not treated in the same way as food. For example, the bodies were often left to decay for several days before being roasted; the book's descriptions of this were enough to turn my stomach just reading about it, so I can only imagine what it's like in person. They ate not out of hunger or desire, but out of a sense of duty, of compassion for the loved ones of the deceased. To them, burying the dead in the ground was a shocking offense—why would you stick the remains of someone you loved in the cold, wet dirt?

When the topic of cannibalism comes up, people often point to disease as a rational, non-taboo-based reason for why it's a terrible idea. Kuru is transmitted by prions, and used to be widespread among the Fore people of Papua New Guinea; there's evidence to suggest it came about because one individual spontaneously developed the disease, and then after that person's death it spread to those who ate their flesh (brain tissue especially), and so on through the group.

But the broader truth is that prion-based diseases can be acquired from the brains of a variety of animals, not only humans. The flesh of our own species is not inherently riddled with diseases waiting to strike down those who transgress by eating their kin. It *can* happen...but so can trichinosis. In the end, the main reasons for not engaging in cannibalism are cultural: we see it as an atrocity, rather than a normal part of victory in battle or the funerary process.

And because we see it as an atrocity, it's incredibly difficult to build it into a setting. Your reader's sense of revulsion will prime them to read it as a marker of evil or primitivism; you'll have to work overtime to get them to see it any other way. Which skews your story: if you weren't writing a story About Cannibalism before, well you are now. You can't just slip in a background reference about how three days after your hero's mentor died, the town dug up his corpse and ate it. The idea derails everything around it.

But that doesn't mean it's impossible to write about. Jo Walton's *Tooth and Claw* transposes the concerns of nineteenth-century Victorian novels to a society of dragons, where they literally eat their dead in order to grow stronger; there the concept is indeed central to the story. Other authors have done the same thing, albeit rarely. If you decide to do it yourself...I wish you luck.

Mourning

Although the question of what a society does with the bodies of the deceased is a key part of the funerary process, it's hardly the whole story. After all, mourning is as much or more about the living as the dead, with a variety of customs designed to protect them from the spirits of the departed or help them through their grief.

These customs can kick in right away. Several different traditions say you should cover any mirrors in the house where a person has died, either to avoid catching glimpses of the evil spirits attracted by death, or to prevent the spirit of the deceased from being caught in the image. Similarly, you might open the windows in the room where the person died in order to permit the spirit's departure. Some societies mandate that a body should be taken out of the house through a window or an opening cut into the wall, to prevent the ghost from finding its way back through the door; this is similar to the idea of carrying the body out feet-first, so it won't look back and beckon someone else to follow (thus leading to another death). Death is a liminal moment, a crossing of the boundaries between life and the afterlife, so it's unsurprising that there would be many practices to guard against the associated dangers.

For those left behind, there is the process of mourning itself. Modern American expectations tend toward quiet dignity, with the bereaved keeping their composure as best as possible while someone gives a eulogy, but that's hardly universal; in other societies mourning is expected to be demonstrative and loud. People tear their clothing, weep freely, wail, keen, and more. Withholding such behaviors would be an insult to the departed—a sign that you don't really care. In fact, the demonstration of grief might be so important that you hire professional mourners to supplement your display.

Which approach is "better"? I suspect it depends on the society and the individual in question. Maintaining your composure in the face of profound loss can be incredibly difficult... but so can forcing yourself into the ostentatious performance of grief, especially if the deceased is someone you personally loathed.

Personal feelings often have no bearing on the formal customs of mourning, though. Many societies mandate who has to mourn (in the sense of performing specific practices) based on the degree and nature of kinship to the departed. In Judaism, for example, the key figures are related within one degree: parents, children, siblings, and spouses. These are the people expected to sit shiva, i.e. observe a fixed seven-day mourning period. By contrast, strict Confucian ideology sometimes forbade anyone to mourn the death of an immature child, because it was considered wrong for people to show such honor and respect to someone beneath them in the hierarchy: it's supposed to flow from child to parent, not the other way around. Christian communities might forbid mourning suicides, because of their unabsolved sin. Shifting to the far end of the spectrum, the death of a monarch or other major public figure might require entire communities to go into mourning.

Because the formal practice is based on social circumstances rather than emotion, it often persists for a set period of time, as with the aforementioned shiva. Victorian society required much lengthier observance of mourning, at least among the upper classes. Men got off relatively easy, marking their grief with black gloves, hatbands, or armbands, but women had it much harder. Although details of the practice varied through the nineteenth century, widows were expected to be in mourning for something like two years, only lightening to "half-mourning" (with clothes in lavender, grey, or black pinstripe) toward the end.

And that was just for deceased husbands. There were also set mourning periods for parents, children, siblings, aunts and uncles, first cousins, in-laws, and even the in-laws of married children. It's no wonder that some women opted never to come out of mourning clothes: purchasing all the necessary garments and accessories was a significant financial burden, with no guarantee you wouldn't have to put them right back on a week after you took them off. (Of course not everyone would have observed all the niceties for the full length of time; whenever you hear about a cultural practice like this, you always have to remember that what is *expected* and what people actually *do* can be quite different.)

Some societies have required even more stringent responses to loss, especially for widows. In East Asia they might be expected to shave their heads and begin life as Buddhist nuns after their husbands pass. In some parts of India, widows similarly move to temples and spend the remainder of their lives begging for alms. The practice of sati was even more extreme, with widows immolating themselves on their husbands' funeral pyres—theoretically of their own free will. But there's no illusion of free will in the ancient tombs we find around the world, where dead rulers were put to rest surrounded by the bodies of sacrificed wives, slaves, horses, and more.

As with quiet versus ostentatious grieving, formal mourning (of the non-lethal variety) has both its good sides and its bad. People in that state are often not expected to carry out all their usual tasks, which can give them some desperately-needed respite, and a structured transition back to normal life can be a source of comfort and assistance—better than being caught in the limbo of not knowing when it's socially acceptable to move on. On the other hand, being barred from participating in normal activities, especially the fun ones that might lighten your spirit, can make the experience of loss more crushing, and the formal return to daily routine might come far too late—or far too soon.

Finally, there's the material culture of death. Tombs,

gravestones, and other markers of the final resting place provide a focal point for mourning, as do memorial tablets or ancestral altars in the home. It's been common for millennia to bury people with grave goods, for reasons ranging from utility in the afterlife, to demonstration of the dead person's importance, to taboos that prohibit any living person from continuing to use those items. Other things are made for the use of the bereaved: going back to the Victorians and their obsession with mortality, you find commemoration of the deceased taking the shape of locks of hair, portraits of the dead, photographs of same (either resting peacefully or posed as if they were still alive), and more. Death masks might be sculpted images made for the coffin, as you see in Egyptian burials, or wax or plaster casts taken directly from the corpse, kept around after burial.

This really only scratches the surface of mourning customs. In the Chinese TV show *Nirvana in Fire* (aka *Lang ya bang*), there's a plot point built around one of the characters avoiding the direct use of the hanzi from his deceased parents' names. There are also all the rituals that may come after death—but those often have to do with the afterlife. For that, continue on to the next essay.

The Afterlife

Finishing out the discussion of death and the culture surrounding it (at least for now): what happens to a person after they die?

Actually, there are two questions to answer here. One is what people *believe* happens after you die; the other is what *really* happens. They may not be the same thing. You don't necessarily have to answer the second question—many stories don't require it—but this being speculative fiction, you *can* choose to answer it definitively. And for some kinds of stories, you have to.

Roughly speaking, you can break the possibilities for what happens after death into four broad categories.

1) Nothing. When you die, that's it; you're gone, and nothing persists afterward. This is generally the position held by atheists, but I'm not aware of any religions with such a belief.

2) Reincarnation. After you die, your spirit is born again in a new body. Your next life may be affected by your actions in the previous (i.e. your karma), but you may or may not remember anything of that previous life. Many religions that believe in reincarnation also say you get wiped clean of memories in between, as part of the cycle, but some hold that it's possible to retrieve at least some of those memories. Reincarnation is strongly associated with Asian religions, but various sects within Abrahamic religions have also promoted the idea.

3) Afterlife. Call it Heaven, Hell, Purgatory, Sheol, Hades,

Elysium, Tartarus, Valhalla, Niflheim, Xibalba, Mictlan, Diyu, Duat, Yomi, or any one of a dozen other names; it's the resting place of souls after they die. Often there are many possibilities within a single belief system, and where you wind up depends (as above) on your actions in life. But that doesn't always mean there's an afterlife for good people and an afterlife for bad ones; sometimes the manner of your death determines where you go, as with Valhalla and Fólkvangr (each of which claimed half of those who died in battle) or Tlalocan (which claimed those who died of causes linked to the rain god Tlaloc).

4) Ghosts. Maybe you don't go anywhere at all: you stay right here on earth, visible all the time or only some of the time, able to interact with the world or not. Often, but not always, ghosts have unfinished business, and when that is resolved, they move on.

Of course you can mix and match these things in various ways, e.g. with ghosts moving on to reincarnation or an afterlife once the reason for their haunting is dealt with, or souls spending some amount of time in an afterlife before they are ready for reincarnation, or foul magics that allow for the possibility that a soul can be utterly destroyed. Some views of nirvana amount to nearly the same thing, but in a positive way, with a soul ceasing to have independent, defined existence once it's freed from the cycle of rebirth.

Theological discussions will have to wait for a future volume (or more than one); for now, the interesting thing is how these beliefs affect the way people build culture around death. If you believe in ghosts, for example, there will be customs in place to prevent them from lingering, as we saw in the previous essay. But where this really kicks in is with belief in reincarnation and the afterlife, because there are all kinds of ways the living can try to assist the dead.

This is one of the reasons grave goods are so widespread of a practice. Whether it's coins on the eyelids to pay the ferryman across the underworld river or food and tools to use in an afterlife that's exactly like this one, people put objects in graves not because they wanted to waste wealth, but because they believed the dead would need those things later. (The wasting of wealth was a real issue, though; that's why Egyptian religion developed the idea that in the underworld, a tiny model of a thing would be just as good as the thing itself. Tiny models are a *lot* cheaper.)

You can also help a person spiritually as well as materially, through rituals performed after death. People often pray for the deceased, recite sutras, learn the Torah, etc. in order to lessen their suffering in Hell (whatever name it may go by in the local religion), shorten their time in Purgatory or between lives, or otherwise bestow benefits on them. Doing such things can be a way to accumulate spiritual merit for yourself at the same time—or, if you're rich, you can pay for somebody else to do it on your behalf, funding a chantry to recite masses for the dead or a scriptorium to copy out sutras.

Other rituals are performed at set times. Japanese Buddhist customs may involve a number of memorial services, e.g. on the seventh, forty-ninth, and hundredth day after death; in Judaism you might unveil the tombstone of the deceased seven or thirty days after the funeral, or on the anniversary. In some cases the timing of such rituals is based on beliefs regarding the soul's journey through the underworld to judgment, with assistance coming at key moments.

Then, of course, you have the yearly holidays: the Day of the Dead, All Souls' Day, the Bon Festival or Ghost Festival, Samhain, and so on. Many cultures have believed in a specific time when the worlds of the living and the dead draw closer together, which is a good (or sometimes a *necessary*) opportunity to honor your deceased relatives. Even without that belief, many countries commemorate the deaths of famous leaders or other beloved public figures, not out of any supernatural belief, but simply because it is a good time to recall their achievements and contributions to society.

As with so many things in speculative fiction, this only tends to show up when it's plot-relevant: a ghost is haunting the characters, or your hero is literally transported to hell. But it should be much more pervasive than that, because belief regarding the afterlife permeates the way we speak. If you don't believe in any kind of hell, will you damn someone to it?

Watching a Korean drama, I saw one of the characters saying "she must have saved the country in a previous life" as a way of explaining the heroine's good fortune. Things like that can play a role in the story, even if the actual afterlife doesn't.

Your Money's Worth

One of the patron rewards I offer is the opportunity to ask me worldbuilding questions. A patron of mine asked about money, and that led to the whole next series of essays.

In fantasy games and quite a few novels, money almost always consists of copper, silver, gold, and (sometimes) platinum. Ten coppers to a silver, ten silvers to a gold, etc. While this is easy to remember and use, it is *phenomenally* inaccurate to how money generally works in the real world.

Sure, in the U.S. we have copper(-colored) coins, silver(-colored) coins, and if you get a Sacagawea dollar, gold(-colored) coins. But we don't call them coppers, silvers, and gold: we call them pennies, nickels, dimes, quarters, dollars. The names of our coins only partially overlap with the actual units of currency they represent; a dollar coin is worth one dollar, but a dime is worth ten cents, not ten pennies. And while our currency is decimal, our coins aren't; there are ten dimes to a dollar, but twenty nickels, or only four quarters.

Let's back up for a second and talk about what money actually *is*.

Trade originally happened on a barter system: you give me milk from your cow, and in exchange I'll give you grain from my field. I'll probably discuss barter more in a future volume, but for now let's skip ahead to the stage where people started using quantities of Valuable Substance as markers for the value of other things.

I phrase it that way because the Valuable Substance in question can vary wildly. It isn't always gold, or even metal. Cowrie shells were used as money for centuries in a wide swath of Africa; cocoa beans served the same purpose in Mesoamerica. In speculative fiction, the Valuable Substance could be whatever "unobtanium" is relevant to the world you've built. In a desert post-apocalypse, it might be water. Basically, as long as people agree that a thing has value, and as long as it's neither so rare that nobody can get hold of it, nor so ubiquitous that there's no reason to value it, you can say people use it as currency.

Metal does offer some distinct virtues in this regard. It's relatively durable; it's also malleable, which means you can make units that are bigger or smaller or more stackable or different shapes, instead of having to pile up more beans or shells to represent greater value. You can alloy it with other metals, too, and once you get scientifically advanced enough, you can assay things to figure out their composition, which helps when you need to determine the "real" value of the coin.

As for that composition, I think gold and silver have historically been the most common, but copper and bronze are also fairly frequent, and any metal or alloy can theoretically work: iron, tin, etc. These days aluminum is cheap and disposable, but obtaining it in pure form requires fairly advanced technology; we didn't figure out how to do that until the nineteenth century, and in the late Victorian period it was more valuable than gold. So in the right setting, you could easily have a society where your D&D-style murderhobos kill the villain and are rewarded with a treasure chest full of aluminum coins!

The rabbit hole of "value" and how it's calculated is a deep one, so rather than falling down it right now, let's get back to that question of coinage and its organization. I am reminded of the following footnote from Neil Gaiman and Terry Pratchett's *Good Omens*:

> Two farthings = One Ha'Penny. Two ha'pennies = One Penny. Three pennies = A Thrupenny Bit.

Two Thrupences = A Sixpence. Two Sixpences = One Shilling, or Bob. Two Bob = A Florin. One Florin and One Sixpence = Half a Crown. Four Half Crowns = Ten Bob Note. Two Ten Bob Notes = One Pound (or 240 pennies). One Pound and One Shilling = One Guinea.

If you wade through the math, you'll find that a shilling is worth twelve pence, and there are twenty shillings to a pound. Even laying aside the lack of decimalization, you might ask, why all the intervening elements? Why not just have coins worth one penny, one shilling, and one pound, and dump all this nonsense of thrupence and sixpence and florins and half crowns and guineas—not to mention the groats and nobles and angels that fell out of use along the way?

There are lots of reasons, ranging from the influence of foreign money (florins were originally minted in Florence, and caused other countries to mint their own equivalents) to the gradual creep of inflation (a penny used to be a meaningful unit of wealth; now it's an annoyance) to the utility of having finer gradations of value. But underlying all of those is the fundamental fact that this system is the end product of *centuries* of accreted revisions, most of them made with an eye toward concerns other than "what's a nice easy system to calculate?"

Narratively speaking, decimalized currency is the most plausible when it's found in a culture that is well-planned and well-organized in other respects. (Or any other consistent numerical approach: Mesoamerican societies were vigesimal, i.e. base 20.) The French revolutionary calendar was so determined to decimalize everything, they not only made decimal currency but also ten-day weeks and even ten-hour days. Systems that have grown over time, on the other hand, are more likely to be ad hoc messes, as seen in the British example above.

But there's a virtue that comes with the "ad hoc mess" approach—at least from the perspective of a writer. If I say that my character buys a meat pie from a street vendor for a cent and then a hat for ten cents, there will be some readers who immediately trip up on the question of whether those values make sense relative to one another: should the hat be more expensive, or less? Whereas if I say that she spends a rasade on the meat pie and three farinzes on the hat, you have no way of checking my math. I still have to pay *some* attention to it, because if later on I say she obtains a horse for one farinze, then either that was a bloody expensive hat, the horse is a swaybacked nag that will keel over one block down the street, or I screwed up. But I have a lot more leeway in naming the prices of things and how much wealth the characters have to throw around, because the conversion rates could be anything.

So: not only is the ad hoc approach more realistic, but it's also more forgiving on a narrative level. Ditch your ten coppers to a silver, and come over to the far more interesting world of farthings, sixpences, and guineas!

Follow the Money

If you go into a store today and buy something, you're almost certainly doing it one of two ways: either you're handing over one or more pieces of paper with no intrinsic value to speak of, or you're handing over nothing at all, merely swiping or inserting or tapping and then voilà, they give you stuff.

How did we get here, from the gold and silver coins of yore?

In the last essay I talked about paying for things with Valuable Stuff, of which gold and silver are common examples. This is what economists call *commodity money*. That is, the money is made from a commodity, something considered to be intrinsically valuable, apart from its role as a medium of exchange. Originally people handed around lumps of gold and judged their value by weight; then things got standardized, first with ingots (like the gold bars in Fort Knox), then with coins.

But commodity money has a problem, which is that it's a pain in the neck to carry around. Maybe literally: you could sprain something trying to lift a chest full of gold coins. When you see one in a movie that's the size of a footlocker and filled to the brim, you should laugh. Real strongboxes were generally small not only because it gave them greater structural integrity against someone trying to bash the lid in, but because that meant you could actually move them when you needed to.

For poor people this might not be much of an issue,

because they didn't have a lot of coins to begin with, but rich people? They weren't going to stroll down the street with a hundred gold coins in their belt pouch. It would bruise their leg with every swing and try to pull their belt right off their body. When they wanted to buy something expensive from a shop, therefore, a lot of the time they didn't actually hand over the cash; they just promised somebody would bring it by later.

This is the origin of credit. The Latin word *creditus* means "trusted;" granting someone credit means granting them trust, believing that they'll pay their debts later. (Some of them did. A lot of them didn't. At least not until after their creditors hounded them to the ends of the earth.) And this could operate not only in a business establishment, but in situations like a game of cards. Young Lord NoLuck wagers a hundred pounds on his hand; it turns out to be not quite as good as he hoped, and now he owes his opponent, Sir Quickfingers. Since he's bloody well not carrying a stake of that magnitude around with him, he writes out and signs a note: "Lord NoLuck owes one hundred pounds."

Here's where it gets interesting. Maybe Sir Quickfingers owes a few debts of his own. He doesn't have the money to pay them...but he has this note from Lord NoLuck. Rather than trying to squeeze the money out of his buddy, then paying his own debts, he hands over the note. Maybe to an honest merchant; maybe to Billy Bruiser, who gives Sir Quickfingers ninety for it (Billy's gotta eat, after all), and then scandalizes the town by showing up on Lord NoLuck's doorstep demanding his due. What with one thing and another, that piece of paper with Lord NoLuck's handwriting on it is now operating almost as if it were actual money, the hundred pounds one presumes— or at least hopes—Lord NoLuck has in his strongbox at home.

Such an approach only works for as long as the person has credit, i.e. is trusted to pay their debts. If they have a history of failing to do so, or you get beyond the sphere of people who know who they are, that piece of paper is as worthless as their promises.

Which is why in the long term this stopped being a game played by individuals, with ad hoc notes scribbled here and there, and started becoming the purview of larger and more stable institutions: governments and banks. Store your piles of extremely heavy metal with the bank, where they have thick walls and stout doors and guys with weapons to protect it, and conduct most or all of your transactions with pieces of paper that stand in for the Valuable Substance.

This is called *representative money*, and it's actually a very old idea—older than coinage, in fact—because these things are rarely as linear in their development as a brief essay would suggest. But there's a key thing to note about representative money in the strict sense, which is that the thing it represents *is still valuable*. Those banknotes used to be redeemable for the piles of metal, if for some reason you really wanted to lug all that weight around. The gold standard, the silver standard, bimetallism—these are different ways of backing the value of paper money. Because, the thought went, of course there needed to be *something* of actual worth involved. Otherwise, why should that paper be worth anything?

And yet, here we are today, paying for stuff with pieces of paper that have no intrinsic value to speak of and don't represent anything valuable, either. That's *fiat money*, from the Latin verb for "let it be done": money that's worth something simply because we as a society have said it's so. It's a great big game of make-believe. And when people stop believing...well, that's when you get exciting types of economic collapse I'm not really qualified to speak on.

So why do I bring this up in the context of worldbuilding? Because in speculative fiction, the middle part of this chain seems to vanish. Fantasy societies use metal commodity money; far-future science fictional societies use "credits," abstract units that often lack any physical representation at all; and stories set in the present day or near to it use fiat money of the type you and I are accustomed to. You rarely see individual credit playing much of a role, unless the setting is sixteenth to nineteenth century Europe, where dissolute young men are forever being chased by their creditors You rarely see representative money, with its promissory notes issued by trustworthy institutions, even though the idea is ancient. Hell, the first documented attempt at fiat money was during the eleventh century, in China—but we think of the idea as too modern to pass muster in a pre-modern society.

But contrary to what *Dungeons and Dragons* and countless video games would have you believe, people vary rarely walked around with dozens of coins in their pockets, much less hundreds. We developed much more convenient systems. And contrary to what a lot of science fiction would have you believe, there's a great deal of utility in physical objects whose wanderings cannot be so easily traced. If the government installs trackers in every chit, somebody's going to invent representative substitutes for those chits, so you can conduct your shady business with more discretion. Those forgotten types are useful; I'd like to see them used.

All That Glitters Is Not Gold

Possibly the most unrealistic thing about money in fantasy is that it almost always just *works*.
   Early in the novel *Quicksilver*, Neal Stephenson—who has a gift for turning damn near anything into a scene—has a scene wherein a merchant, the protagonist Daniel Waterhouse, and Isaac Newton (who would later go on to head the Royal Mint) bargain over a purchase. But this isn't your typical fantasy bargaining scene where the merchant asks for twenty and Newton offers ten and they agree on fifteen: no, first the debate is over the currency in which Newton will pay (French, German, English), and then over the actual shillings Newton produces from his pocket.
   Because in the world of pre-modern coinage, money is anything but simple and straightforward.
   Stephenson's scene is a guided tour of some of the problems. In theory, coinage solves one of the core problems of commodity money: if someone pays you with silver, how can you be sure how much silver you've received? You can weigh it…but that requires reliable scales (which is a hurdle all on its own) and fairly sophisticated metallurgical knowledge to be sure whether the volume and the mass line up as they should. Coinage was supposed to be a solution to that problem: stamp out regular objects of known value, and everyone can take them at (quite literally) face value.
   Except it isn't that simple. When were those coins minted?

Waterhouse, bargaining in 1665, has in his pocket a shilling from the reign of Elizabeth I, who died in 1603. Newton's are mostly from James I, her successor, but he also has an Edward VI shilling (died 1553), which might have been issued during the final Great Debasement, when the precious metal content of coinage was greatly reduced. This is an economic tool used by governments to increase their own revenue; after all, if they can produce coins more cheaply, they benefit. But it means that the value of a given denomination suddenly becomes a matter for debate, fluctuating depending on when the coin in hand was minted. Ditto coins from different countries, which may not follow the same metallurgical standard, even if they're theoretically minting coins of the same type.

This same principle drives some types of counterfeiting. With modern fiat money, the issue isn't that a fake twenty-dollar bill has less inherent value than a real one—it's hard to go lower than nil—but rather that it's creating value out of thin air. If you're counterfeiting commodity money, on the other hand, you need to pass something cheap off as valuable instead. If it's cocoa beans you're faking up, you craft them out of clay or wax, but if it's metal, you pretty much use the exact same methods as the government…but illegally.

Sometimes this means coating a brass disk in just enough silver to make it look good; the merchant in Stephenson's scene scratches one coin to see if it changes color, and current U.S. pennies are actually copper-plated zinc. Sometimes it means making coins out of some admixture that will look more or less right, but is worth far less; the merchant also bites one of the "silver" shillings, and declares it "not above fifty percent lead."

Doing this successfully isn't easy. If you want your coins to pass muster for any length of time, you again need sophisticated metallurgical knowledge, to make your counterfeits both cheap and realistic. You need an engraver capable of copying the design used to stamp out real coins—since those designs are, after all, partly an anti-counterfeiting technique. And you need a way to feed your coins into the economy without them being traced easily back to you, because counterfeiting is an *incredibly* serious crime, and one that could often lead to execution.

Why? Because it has the potential to destroy a nation's economy. Official debasement is dangerous enough; it leads to inflation, because the purchasing power of the debased coin has been reduced. But counterfeiting? That destroys confidence in the coinage entirely. The value of an officially debased coin is at least *known*. When fakes circulate among the real, the inherent value of any given coin is uncertain, at least without testing. Merchants may stop accepting that type of coin at all, preferring other denominations or even foreign money, which are seen as more trustworthy. The knock-on effects of this can be huge—and the only novels I've read that take this into account at all are Stephenson's Baroque Cycle (of which *Quicksilver* is the first book) and Tamora Pierce's second Beka Cooper book, *Bloodhound*, where counterfeiters play a large role in the plot.

And other than Stephenson, I'm not sure I've seen anyone bring up the issue of "clipping," even though it was quite widespread. Ever wondered why the edges of some coins are milled, i.e. have tiny incised lines? It's because milling is an anti-clipping measure. Take a typical sixteenth-century English shilling, stamped by hand out of a disc of (more or less) silver. Its edge is blobby and irregular. Nobody will notice if you shave a tiny bit off, right? That tiny bit isn't worth much…but if you shave the edges off enough coins, pretty soon you have a pile of (more or less) silver, in addition to your original pile of shillings. Take those shavings to an unethical silversmith, and he'll pay you for them, then melt them down for his own use. Illegal as hell, of course, but it's an easy way to profit. The result is a bunch of coins in circulation that have been pared down to a ludicrous degree: the merchant in *Quicksilver* declares Newton's Edward VI shilling to be "nearly triangular." The reasons why a shilling may not be worth a shilling keep piling up.

This is why Isaac Newton, the renowned scientist even schoolchildren have heard of, was appointed to head the Royal Mint. Ensuring the value of money is a *really complicated task*, and one that's vital to the health of the nation. You need systems for controlling the production process, for discouraging clipping, for tracking down coiners, i.e. people making counterfeit money. Without those measures in place, you get conversations like the one Stephenson wrote, where bargaining is as much a debate over the value of a coin as the value of the item it's being used to buy.

Most of us are not going to write out those conversations in full, because most of us aren't writing novels where such economic matters are a central concern. But the issues are still good ones to keep in mind, because the problems they present may come up in passing. Rather than the boring and clichéd "meet in the middle" approach to bargaining we've seen a thousand times, have the merchant agree to drop the price if the buyer pays in coins from a more recent minting, or in the currency of a neighboring country instead of the local one. Have a character take the desperate measure of shaving the edges off their cash to stretch it just a little further. When you need political scandal, have the Master of the Mint be caught embezzling from his job; when you need a throwaway reference to the queen meeting with some official on a matter of business, drop in a reference to potential debasement or the annual Trial of the Pyx (to ensure the integrity of the nation's coinage). It all lends that extra touch of reality, for not a lot of effort.

Signs of Power

We've talked already about how we show respect to one another, and we've started talking about money. Putting them together, let's talk about the things that signal HEY, YOU SHOULD SHOW RESPECT TO ME.

There are a number of items that traditionally mark someone out as having particular authority. Two crop up in particular when we're talking about royalty: 1) thrones and 2) crowns. In fact, they're so central to the concept of royalty that they can serve as metonymy for the sovereign or even the entire royal government, as when we talk about having the ear of the throne (i.e. the king will listen to what you have to say) or the Crown imposing a new tax. When we talk about installing a new sovereign, the most common words for this are "enthronement" and "coronation" (though other terms do get used, like "proclamation"). So it's understandable that they loom so large in the imagination.

But thrones and crowns are far from the only objects associated with authority. If you go to see the "crown jewels" of the United Kingdom, you'll find yourself staring at everything from swords to robes to orbs to trumpets. Because when you get down to it, pretty much anything can be a symbol of power, if people agree to view it that way.

That doesn't mean regalia is random, though. Quite a lot of it is meant to be worn, because putting splendid adornments on yourself is a good way to impress people: clothing like robes or capes or shoes, or jewelry like crowns, rings, belt buckles, or chains of office. Some are objects that at least theoretically have utilitarian use, whether it's weapons (swords, maces, staves/scepters, daggers; almost certainly derived from the days when you used those things to *win* power) or seals (for marking documents as official and authoritative) or fans or flywhisks or sacred texts.

Of course, many of those are so heavily decorated—not to mention heavy—that you would never actually employ them; ceremonial swords tend to be encrusted with gems to the point where they almost look more painful to the wielder than the target. So there may not be a whole lot of difference between those and the objects that are purely symbolic, like the widespread European *globus cruciger*, the orb surmounted with a cross, which represents Christ's dominion over the world. (And therefore the holder's dominion over said world on Christ's behalf.)

Then you have the stuff that holds the monarch instead of being held by them. Thrones aren't the only form of important seating. In Yoruba it's a stool. In Mesoamerica, where chairs weren't so common, the mat someone sat on could be the symbol of their authority, and before Japan started flooring entire rooms with tatami, those were portable items used as seating for the highest-ranking people present. Renaissance European monarchs often had a canopy of estate over their non-throne chairs—which may have served a practical purpose by protecting them from bugs falling out of the rafters, but also provided a splendid "heaven" over their heads. In other parts of the world, umbrellas serve the same purpose.

Or take conveyances. I have no idea what royal carriages looked like in the English past, but judging by the bling-tastic Lord Mayor of London's state coach, they must have been pretty spectacular. Modify the vehicles as necessary for local tech level and environment: in ancient Egypt the pharaoh would have a royal barge to float up and down the Nile, while in ancient India it might be a chariot.

As these examples suggest, a lot of what makes something a symbol of power and status is the wealth it displays. Gold, silver, precious gems, exotic wood, or fine craftsmanship all communicate the message that the person so adorned or conveyed must be really important. But what about the Stone of Scone, which is nothing more than a chunk of rock with a rough cross carved into it and a couple of rings to help you lift the bloody thing? What about the Holy Lance in Vienna, which despite having a piece of gold slapped on is basically just a steel blade with an iron nail accessory? What about Kusanagi, the sacred sword of Japan, so shrouded in ritual and secrecy that whether it even still exists is open to question?

As the orb-and-cross example above suggests, symbolism plays a role. Giving someone a "key to the city" nods back to the days when cities were surrounded by walls, whose gates might actually be locked with a key; even if there are no longer any walls or gates to put the key in, it's still a way of representing the freedom to come and go whenever you please, or to control other peoples' access. (Many of my examples here have been royal, but I'll note that a woman's ring of keys for doors and chests in her household was often a very practical sign of her power.) But when you get down to it, the primary answer for why a given thing represents status and power is often *history*.

Sure, the Stone of Scone is a fairly plain rock. But it's a plain rock that supposedly served as a pillow for the Israelite patriarch Jacob and later became the coronation stone of Scottish monarchs before the English stole it in the thirteenth century and built it into the chair they used for their own coronations and didn't give it back until 1996. Like the iron nail in the Holy Lance (supposedly a relic of Christ's crucifixion), the intrinsic value isn't what matters; it's the connection to important people and events. It doesn't matter whether the common people ever get to see Kusanagi; that sword, along with the mirror Yata no Kagami and the necklace of comma-shaped jewels Yasakani no Magatama, has been part of the enthronement ceremony for the Japanese emperor since the ninth century, and the origins of those three items connect the imperial line back to their divine ancestor, the sun goddess Amaterasu.

So from a narrative standpoint, it doesn't matter so much whether a given object has precedent in reality as a symbol of authority. The real question is whether it fits into its own context. Special shoes to prevent special feet from touching the ground, a sacred bell whose ringing begins and ends vital ceremonies, a splendid belt that symbolizes the world and thus positions its wearer as the center of that world—nearly anything can work, so long as it has a rationale the reader can believe in.

Sumptuary Laws

Any society that has ways of marking certain people out as having power and authority—which is most of them—will also have ways of restricting those signs to the people who ought to have them.

There are penalties for impersonating a police officer; you can't dress up in a uniform and flash around a fake badge without consequences. Similarly, an army lieutenant who decides to pin on a general's stars is going to be in a world of hurt. In the Mayan Quiché kingdom, the top officials known as the Keeper of the Mat, Keeper of the Reception House Mat, Lord Minister, and Crier to the People were permitted canopies according to their rank: four, three, two, and one, respectively, and bad things would have happened to anybody who tried to break that rule.

But this goes well beyond claiming specific authority you don't have. I mentioned before that one of the ways to say "I'm important" is to wear or carry or use items that are made from precious materials, or have expensive workmanship. That works fine so long as the main metric of social class is how much money you have; someone working three minimum-wage jobs just to pay their rent can't pretend to be the upper crust of New York society because they flat-out can't *afford* the trappings that would allow them to try. Historically speaking, though, lots of cultures have treated class as a matter of birth or achievement, and have frowned heavily on people trying to use money to buy their way into the upper strata.

Those cultures tend to have special regulations called *sumptuary laws*. You mostly hear about these in the context of clothing, but they apply to any form of consumption: food, furniture, the size of your entourage, even the way you build your house. Such laws reserve certain types of luxury only for the "right" kind of people, and impose fines or other punishments for individuals who overstep their bounds.

Let's start with clothing, since the examples there are so abundant. Sumptuary laws may govern the use of certain fabrics (no silk for the hoi polloi!), dyes (Tyrian purple was hugely significant in ancient Rome), garments (Heian Japan restricted hat types by bureaucratic rank), cuts (restriction of necklines or sleeve lengths or nearly anything else), embroidery (limiting both quantity and subject matter), jewelry (Islamic sumptuary laws discourage men from wearing gold), and so forth.

What's interesting here is that the purpose of the law may be to maintain the power of the elite…but it may also be to keep the non-elite down. Banning native dress in a subjugated population, or requiring disfavored groups like prostitutes or members of religious minorities to wear markers of their status, also helps to maintain the structure of the society.

When it comes to food, sumptuary laws may be about protecting certain resources for the use of the elite. This is kind of what's at work with medieval English laws against the taking of game in royal forest; it's also a prohibition against commoners eating venison and such, at least in theory. But it also shows up in situations where allowing widespread consumption would have the *positive* effect of encouraging trade, because restricting access to imported foodstuffs (coffee, tea, spices, oranges, and so on) turns those things into a privilege for the upper crust This often carries a moralizing element: there are endless historical documents inveighing against the fecklessness of the poor, spending their limited coin on tea or whatever. (And if you think this sort of law has died out in modern times, check out the regulations governing what you are and are not allowed to spend food stamps on in the United States. Our Puritanical background is still very much with us.)

Sometimes these laws serve a very practical purpose: it makes a great deal of sense to restrict how many followers someone can bring with them when those followers are likely to be armed, or when the host is expected to house and feed the entire group. (On the other hand, why the limitation that a freeborn Greek woman can only be accompanied by one female slave…with an exception for when she's drunk?) But just as often—maybe more so—the elite impose these restrictions simply because they *can*.

Why did Tokugawa Japan forbid the construction of a certain style of gatehouse in the residences of non-samurai? Or the *shoin*-style room, with its precise arrangement of a display alcove, a side desk, and three shelves? Simply because those things were seen as desirable, and therefore telling someone "you can't have it" was a way to exert your power. But of course that is, in its own way, a practical reason, because this kind of social stratification relies on a constant policing of boundaries between the layers. Those three shelves have no inherent value of their own; they only matter as a signifier for a more important struggle.

One the elite frequently lost. The history of sumptuary laws is also a history of them being *broken*. Sometimes they were bent deliberately, with someone being given the explicit right to some luxury as a bribe or reward for service: wearing a sword, embroidering clothing with a royal symbol, eating a special kind of food given to them as a gift. But other times the rules were straight-up flouted. People with money want to use it to buy nice stuff, and people selling nice stuff want money from whoever can give it to them. English peasants poached deer. Japanese merchants used cypress wood in their houses and bribed inspection officials to look the other way.

Pretending to specific authority was relatively rare—the consequences for passing yourself off as royalty or a military officer were usually severe—but enjoying the fruits of higher status happened all the time. Sometimes the penalties weren't even enforced, and when they were, people shrugged them off. It's like breaking the speed limit these days: eh, you might have to pay a speeding ticket occasionally, but the rest of the time you get to enjoy yourself. And that's a bargain human beings are very prone to making.

We all know that status has its benefits. Rather a lot of them, in fact, and the lack of it is rarely a good thing. But it also brings burdens. And when the benefits and the burdens get out of balance, being a person with status can suck in some creative new ways...

Status Without Wealth

In the previous essay I talked about the dynamics that arise when wealth is not (supposed to be) the metric of your rank. But I spoke of it mainly from the direction of people without status having lots of money, rather than from the other side—when rank is accompanied by insufficient cash.

This is the "keeping up with the Joneses" dynamic. Even in the absence of laws requiring the upper classes to wear expensive fabrics or finely-tailored official robes, there's still a weight of expectation saying that you *should*. (Most of the time. There have been puritanical societies, e.g. the actual Puritans, with different views.) In cultures that make a major virtue out of generosity, you're in trouble if you don't throw lavish banquets or give away your possessions to anyone who admires them. Your house must be grand, your entertainments grander. And over time...being important can bankrupt you.

If you don't do it to yourself, someone else may step in. In Renaissance England, the monarch would sometimes go on a "royal progress," i.e. a political road trip around their realm. Being visited by the sovereign was a great honor—so great, in fact, that some people built lavish manors with chambers intended for royal use, which then sat around unused and chewing through maintenance money while their owners tried in vain to attract the king's or queen's eye. But the angle I find especially interesting is when the honor of hosting the progress was used as a means of control, or even punishment.

Because of course you aren't just hosting the monarch: you're hosting their *progress*. Which is to say, an enormous retinue of servants and attendants and hangers-on and the servants and attendants of the hangers-on, all of whom expect a roof over their heads (well, the servants might not) and regular meals and meanwhile their horses are trampling your fields and eating you out of house and home and you didn't need that firewood or coal for this winter, did you?

Hosting a progress could *ruin* a person. So while a close ally of the king or queen might receive a brief visit—enough to shine the light of royal attention on them; not enough to become a burden—a fractious noble might find himself crushed under the weight of a lengthy stay. By the time the progress moved on, that noble barely had enough money left to repair the damage it had done, let alone plot rebellion. It's an elegant way to ruin someone, and look gracious while you're doing it.

Mostly, though, what happened over time is that the basis of aristocratic wealth fell out from under the upper classes. This dynamic crops up in both England and Japan, two countries whose histories I'm pretty familiar with; I bet it happened elsewhere, too. Go back a thousand years or so, and you'll find that land ownership and exploitation is the main source of wealth, via farms, mines, and other such modes of production. Therefore, the people who owned the land (or at least its products) were also the richest, *and* the ones with power.

But over time, that changed. If you want to see this in action, read Neal Stephenson's "System of the World" trilogy; he gets more detailed about the process than you're likely to see anywhere outside of an economic history textbook. Short form is, things like commerce rose in importance while the value of land ownership declined, via everything from overworking the soil to the partition of estates. Cue the rise of mercantile classes—but long-standing prejudices meant that aristocrats were reluctant to sully themselves with money earned from sources other than land or investments.

Run this shift for long enough, and you wind up with rich merchants living the high life, and penniless aristocrats with little of value to their names apart from the names themselves.

Ever wonder why so many of those eighteenth- and nineteenth-century young Englishmen were forever dodging their creditors? In some cases it was because they were truly feckless, but in others it's because the sand was washing out from under their feet. Expectations hadn't yet caught up with the fact that the peerage wasn't as rich as it used to be, so people spent far beyond their long-term means. Even today, you can find English aristocrats hocking their ancestral estates, or turning them into museums in a desperate bid to make the places bring in enough money to cover their upkeep. If their families had no status, it would be easier for them to scale down over the generations, or accept the new economic reality and adapt to commercial demands. But when you're carrying the weight of a title, a lineage, the expectations of your social class...then it isn't so simple.

Which means it's an engine for story. Whether you feel sympathetic to people in that situation or not, it's fodder for everything from romance plots (Impoverished Aristocrat Seeks Wealthy Plebian Bride) to tragedy (shouldn't have gone to that guy for help with your debts...) to intrigue (the horse-trading of political influence for monetary support) and more.

I'll be honest with you all: I kind of loathe economics as a subject. I blame a very bad experience with studying it in high school. But I find myself coming back to it again and again, never in major, plot-centric ways, but as minor touches in the background of a whole bunch of different stories. It lends a note of reality, creates little patches of conflict, gives characters motivations with an extra layer of complexity. So even though my eyes cross at the first mention of GDP, I try to pay attention to certain aspects of the topic—and I like stories that do the same.

The History We Live In

In addition to asking me specific worldbuilding questions, my patrons at a certain level and above have the chance to request essays on certain topics. In this case, the suggestion had to do with conveying historical complexity, which is itself complex enough that it can't be answered in a single piece. When I cast about for a specific angle to hit first, I landed on…architectural history, of all things. (I blame the research reading I had been doing.)

How can buildings convey a sense of history, politics, and change over time?

Let's start with ancient ruins. As any reader of the Memoirs of Lady Trent knows, I have a soft spot for these, and certainly they lend themselves well to fantasy or certain kinds of spacefaring science fiction. Whether it's Stonehenge in England or Karnak in Egypt or Chichén Itzá in Mexico, the remnants of ancient civilizations are a clear sign of time's passage. Is the ethnic group that created them still around, or have they "vanished" through migration, conquest by an outside power, or simply change on so significant a scale they're no longer meaningfully the same people? (Roman and Islamic influence radically altered Egypt, but contrary to the way it's usually described, the Maya didn't disappear; they're just not living in those cities anymore.) Do the local people know what purpose the site originally served, or is it a mystery now, the subject of folkloric invention or scientific investigation?

And what state is the site in, anyway? Some kinds of architecture (stone) survive reasonably well even without maintenance; others (wood) will vanish pretty quickly, leaving behind only traces. The environment will affect this, of course, through erosion and moisture-based decay. But people affect it, too, by stealing away building materials for re-use at other sites. Why go cut new stone from a distant quarry when you could take already-dressed blocks from a nearby abandoned building? Ditto for fired bricks and even large timber beams. If you've ever seen an old ruin in Europe and wondered why it was built out of mortared rubble, you may be seeing the infill of the wall, left behind after the nice facing stones were removed.

Which means you can wind up with fragments in the oddest places. I read an article some time ago about a Norse runestone found serving as the threshold of a farmhouse, and the Rosetta Stone was used as fill when a Mamluk sultan built the site known as Fort Julien or the Fort of Qaitbey. Decorations or inscriptions can signal that components of a structure have been moved from their original location.

This kind of repurposing can happen to whole buildings, too. These days the Hagia Sophia (Ayasofya) in Istanbul is a museum; before that it was a mosque; before that it was a Greek Orthodox basilica. The Pantheon in Rome once honored all the gods, as the name suggests, but in the seventh century it became a Western Christian church instead. Over in Japan, many Buddhist temple properties were once manor houses, donated by some pious aristocrat hoping to better their karma for their next life. And during the English Civil War, Parliamentary forces stabled their horses in the nave of St. Paul's Cathedral in London. Sometimes repurposing happens because the original use has been forgotten, but more often it occurs because that original use is no longer necessary or desired. It can even be a form of ideological warfare, the victor deliberately overwriting the loser's history and habits with their own.

Speaking of victors, buildings can also be a way of commemorating history. Triumphal arches, columns, stelae, and so forth are a really blatant example of this: structures that often serve no practical purpose apart from putting a giant sign on the landscape saying THE DUDE WHO COMMISSIONED THIS WAS AWESOME. Memorials do the same thing, but in a less self-aggrandizing direction.

Nothing says you can't combine advertising with use, though, which is how you get temples, palaces, hospitals, and even smaller things like fountains that bear the name or statue of the wealthy person who arranged for their construction. (And if you don't think a fountain is an important public service, you've never thought about the effort required to obtain water when it isn't piped into your house.) A building may not be only a building; it can also be a reminder of historical figures or grand events, keeping the memory of those things alive in daily life.

Even on a more modest scale, architecture can communicate history through changes in fashion. When I was researching the Onyx Court series, architecture was an inescapable part of how London changed over time. I started with Tudor half-timbered buildings; then, after most of those burned down in the Great Fire of 1666, civil codes mandated the use of much less flammable brick; then the classical inspirations of Palladianism overran the place with their columns and symmetrical facades.

More recently I've been reading about the history of Japanese architecture, with shifts from the early *shinden* style to the later *shoin* style and then the influx of Western materials and methods after the Meiji Restoration. None of which is the kind of thing I'm likely to lecture the reader about in the story—but that doesn't mean it won't show up at the edges. A book on *minkan* (folk) architecture comments on how those buildings came to be seen as dark and lacking in privacy; similar complaints were directed at Tudor buildings. A passing line in a description can convey the sense that such things are old-fashioned by the time of the story. Meanwhile, newfangled styles might be admired as *au courant* or decried as silly fads.

And the driving forces behind those changes? Those convey history. Conquest from the outside, which brings the invader's styles in, or conquest *of* the outside, which inspires a hunger for "exotic" innovations. Increased trade can bring new materials like marble or fine wood, while the loss of external trade during the Tokugawa period influenced Japanese architecture to become more frugal in its use of resources, leading to the minimalist aesthetic we associate with that culture. Country A admiring Country B often means that A begins aping the fashions of B, like the popular kid at school creating a trend for certain articles of clothing.

You don't need a historical lecture to imply these things happened. You just need a throwaway line about Lord Sycophant tearing down his unfashionable Old Dynasty manor to build something in the popular new Usurper style, or a nouveau riche merchant flaunting her wealth with cedar wood imported from the colonies. Your street-side flower-seller might ply her trade at the base of a column from imperial days, and have one-sided conversations with the conquered people carved into its exterior.

Take a look at the world around you. How many buildings commemorate the past in some way? How many retain traces of their previous purpose, through an overlayer of more recent adaptation? Unless you live in a brand-new development (which, to be fair, you may), there's more of it than you might think.

Worldbuilding as a Habit of Thought

It's very possible that some of you have read through this book and despaired, because how can you possibly keep all of these things in mind as you write? In only a single volume, I've already dug into everything from seasonal patterns to the meaning of personal names to counterfeit coinage to divination. In upcoming volumes I'm likely to discuss dueling, cartography, hair care, and how people sleep. The list of cultural details you might incorporate into your setting is essentially endless. Are you supposed to work out every last aspect of the world before you can start writing the story?

Obviously the answer is "no," because working out *every* last detail of the world is impossible. (At least if it's meant to be a realistic-seeming world, rather than some odd surrealist allegory-type thing.) But some people do take an exhaustive approach to this process. Patricia C. Wrede has a set of worldbuilding questions on her site that's even more granular than this Patreon! For some writers, it may work to go through that entire list and answer every last item, maybe even before they start writing.

That isn't what I do, though, and it isn't what I recommend. (Not least because it can turn into a really great tool for procrastination: *I can't write yet, because I haven't yet decided what style of footwear was in fashion a hundred years ago in the capital city!*) Rather, I view Wrede's list of questions—and my New Worlds series—as a tool for training yourself into certain habits of thought.

Think of what happens with your prose over time. For most of us, when we start out writing, we just kind of fling down words as they come to us. But over time we start to notice clichés, stock expressions, images we really love and use way too often, my god how many of my last ten sentences did I start with a participial phrase...so then maybe you spend a while focusing *really hard* on your prose, not letting any sentence slip by unexamined, constantly prodding yourself to find new ways to say things—some of which probably succeed better than others.

Taken too far, this turns you into the proverbial centipede who forgets how to walk the moment he tries to think about how all those legs move. But when you come out the other side of it, your habits have changed: you have a larger stock of images to choose from on the fly, a subconscious awareness of when you're repeating yourself, and every now and then you pause mid-scene to hunt for a better way to construct a key line. Overall, writing more vivid prose has become a thing you do reflexively, rather than one consciously chosen word at a time.

In worldbuilding, the same thing can be true. You're in the middle of a scene in your fantasy novel that features a greedy trader, and when you reach for a descriptor to convey why the viewpoint character finds him so unpleasant, your imagination offers up a stock image: the fat, greasy merchant, whose overweight body is supposed to represent his avarice. Offensive stereotype ahoy! How else can you show this guy's nature, without resorting to "fat = bad"?

Something deep in your subconscious stirs. *Rich merchant. Aristocratic society. Sumptuary laws!* You delete the lines about his weight and instead describe how the fabric or dye or embroidery of his clothing crosses the line that's supposed to separate him from his social superiors. Now his greed is being expressed through behavior, *and* you've added a layer of richness to your world in the process. You don't have to write out the twenty-seven sumptuary laws of that society before you get started; you only need some part of your brain to remember that's a thing, and trot it out when the occasion presents itself.

That's what I mean when I say worldbuilding is a habit of

thought. The more you make yourself aware of the building blocks that make up human culture, the more likely you are to notice when there's an opportunity to do something interesting with one, either in passing or as a major plot point. The more you make yourself aware of the different shapes and sizes and colors and materials these building blocks can have, the more vivid and memorable your world will be, because it isn't constructed out of the same identical red bricks the reader has seen in a hundred other novels. You stop thinking in defaults, start thinking in specifics.

It can still help to work on this as a focused exercise, the same way it can help with your prose. Sit down with Wrede's questions and see how many of them you have answers to and how many you don't; see how many of those answers are the first thing that came to mind, instead of something further off the beaten path. Maybe one of those questions will give you a really cool idea, and when you think about that idea it changes other parts of your world, and the next thing you know your story has developed a whole new dimension that wouldn't have been there if you hadn't put thought into the sewage system of your Mars terraforming colony.

But the rest of the time, just let this sink into the background, a new habit that shapes how you tell your stories.

Bricolage

Sometimes a secondary world setting is pretty clearly a primary world location and time period with some names changed. I've done this myself, with the Memoirs of Lady Trent; Scirland is not quite England (starting with the fact that the dominant religion is based on rabbinic Judaism instead of Christianity), but it's *mostly* England. Guy Gavriel Kay has done this a lot, and so has Tamora Pierce. When you're writing something like of that type, the process of worldbuilding consists of researching your source, and then deciding which bits you're going to change.

Building a new setting is different. You're never going to make anything that is One Hundred Percent Brand New; there will always be echoes and similarities to other stories and the real world. But if you're not trying to replicate a specific source, then you're left in a middle zone best described by the French word *bricolage*.

I usually see this translated into English as "tinkering," but I think "macgyvering" comes closer (after the 1980s TV series, rebooted in 2016). Bricolage is the process of assembling something from assorted bits and pieces. The term has been adopted into a wide swath of fields; I encountered it in anthropology, where it's used to discuss how societies adapt to problems by cobbling together novel solutions from the cultural institutions and ideologies they already possess. In worldbuilding, it's the process by which you take what you know about different kinds of governments and religions and foodways and clothing and fighting styles and marriage customs, and you pick some out and glue them together into a setting.

This is unavoidable. As soon as you enter the realm of speculative fiction, you're having to invent new things: social structures that encompass vampires or teleportation technology or the fact that everyone lives on ships in the middle of the sea. And then there's the worldbuilding we do, not because the speculative element demands it, but simply because we like imagining different things. So I decide that, okay, in this story I'm going to have an empire with a deified ruler, a bit like Egypt or Rome, but with a caste system more like India, only I want the system to be a little permeable so let's introduce an examination system of some kind like China had...and what I wind up with doesn't quite look like Egypt or Rome or India or China, but if you poke at the seams you might be able to guess at the pieces of fabric I used to make my quilt.

So here's the difficult question: where's the line between that and cultural appropriation?

One of the major problems with cultural appropriation is that you get writers cherry-picking the "fun" bits out of a real-world society and plonking them down in the middle of a different setting, without any of the underpinnings that supported them in their original home. Maybe I think Japan is cool, so I write something with samurai and katana and ninja, but I've decided I want to cross-breed that with Vikings and Aztecs, so I slap those bits of Japan down in a tropical forest populated by tall blond people and I throw in some mead to go with the blood sacrifice or whatever, and isn't it shiny?

Well, maybe to the writer. But to the people for whom those amputated details are their own culture—people who have frequently seen their culture misrepresented and commodified by people who don't understand it—the result isn't so much shiny as painful.

Our lives would be a lot easier if the line between bricolage and appropriation were sharp and easy to spot. Unfortunately, it isn't that simple. I can't answer the question of the best way to do this in a single blog post; I couldn't even answer it in a series, because the answer is going to vary from writer to writer and reader to reader, and a lot of the most important things are being said by people more on the marginalized end of that transaction than I am. There are a great many essays out there you can go read to explore this issue—I recommend looking into Nisi Shawl's work as a starting point.

What I *can* say is that, much as with derivative works and copyright law, transformation can be your friend. Instead of using a thing in an obviously recognizable but amputated form, change it and integrate it with the rest of your setting. Katana are Japanese: no question about it. But the general notion of a heavy, single-edged blade that is usually wielded two-handed is not somehow inherently tied to Japanese genetics. Call it something other than a katana. Give its decorative components, like the guard and the sheath, a different aesthetic. Think about the ideological weight given to that blade in your invented society; if the rest of that society isn't anything like Japan, then the way those swords fit into the culture won't be the same, either.

Eventually you're describing your setting to a friend and instead of saying "they fight with katana," you tell your friend about this cool sword and the role it plays and when your friend asks what it looks like, you say "sort of like a katana." Because what you have at that point isn't precisely a katana anymore, just as the empire I described above is sort of like Egypt or Rome and sort of like India and sort of like China, but in the end it isn't really any of those things. I drew on the underlying principles (deification, caste, theoretically meritocratic advancement) rather than specific external manifestations (pharaohs, kshatriyas, imperial examinations). When you do that, you open up space to do things like add another caste or have the examinations serve more purposes than merely selecting officials for the civil service, without it coming across as a failure on your part to understand how those institutions worked in history.

The more you understand those underlying principles, the more effectively you can do this. And that's why I recommend reading so broadly in anthropology, history, and related fields: not only because it provides you with possible inspiration, but because it helps you develop that conscious and subconscious understanding of how societies fit together, and what you have to do to produce a coherent result from disparate parts.

Liminality

Liminality has come up in these essays before, particularly in the context of rites of passage. But it's a concept with much broader application than that one area, and since this essay originally ran a few days before New Year's Eve—the transition from one year to the next—it was a good time to pull the idea of liminality out and take a closer look at it: what it means, and what you can do with it.

The word comes from the Latin for threshold, *limen*. Liminality is the quality possessed by things that sit on or transgress the boundaries between things. And since we're very much wired to categorize our world, to put things into boxes and then use those boxes to sort and process our experiences, liminal things are…well, there are a lot of words you could use to describe them. Unsettling. Confusing. Powerful. Dangerous.

Interesting!

Liminality is a *fabulous* concept to play around with in fiction. It's especially great to use in fantasy, because you can work it into all kinds of magic and supernatural things, building the idea that they carry more force because of their liminal associations. After all, if that's true folklorically, why can't it be true fictionally? But you don't need the story to feature actual spiritual events for liminal associations to play a part. The power of the idea is psychological, too.

Since I mentioned New Year's Eve, let's start off with the ways you can time events in your story to make use of this effect. Having an event take place at a transitional moment of some kind, a period of time that transgresses boundaries, can help create the feeling that your characters or your world are a little bit unmoored, ready for transformation.

Why is midnight the witching hour? Because under our time system, it's the boundary between one day and the next. Dawn and dusk are also good, the shift from light to dark and back again. Ditto the equinoxes and the solstices, or eclipses, the transgression of one celestial object on the light of another. In the Mesoamerican calendar, the months work out to 360 days; then there are five intercalary days (like our Leap Day) to fill it out, which used to be seen as a time of cosmological danger.

You can even make use of it on a more personal scale, the moments in a character's life where they're undergoing a rite of passage or some less formalized transition. There's more than one reason we love to have major story events happen on characters' birthdays. Dramatic interventions occur at weddings (at least fictional ones) not only because that's the romantic equivalent of the "ticking clock, down to the wire" bomb scenario, but also because the bride and groom are unmoored from their usual states, ready for a sudden and life-altering change. The entire tradition of Carnival is based in the notion of a breakdown of boundaries, letting go of your usual identity and social structures: during carnival you can mock authority, violate taboos, and otherwise cut yourself loose.

Or you can have the event happen in a liminal location. Literal doorways, the origin of the word, are obvious candidates, which is why you get things like warding magic at the threshold, or a groom carrying his bride into their new house. So are shorelines, where water meets land. So are the boundaries between kingdoms or other units of land. Parlays between opposing armies often happened on the field between their lines of battle, in the "no man's land" where transformation of the status quo from war to peace or back again became possible. The ocean is liminal; "international waters" belong to no country, and so are prime places for lawless activities, whether that's piracy or gambling, because that's where society breaks down.

There's a major example of this kind of thing in the story of the Welsh hero Lleu Llaw Gyffes: he is unable to be killed during the day or the night, indoors or outdoors, riding or walking, clothed or naked, or by any weapon lawfully made. Sounds like he can't be killed at all, right? But he reveals to his traitorous wife that it can be done...if it happens at dusk, while he is wrapped in a net, standing with one foot on a cauldron and one on a goat, and the weapon is a spear forged while people are at Mass. In short: he can only be killed when he is in a (very thoroughly) liminal state.

Certain things can, in and of themselves, be seen as transgressing or falling outside the symbolic boundaries of our world. The anthropologist Mary Douglas once theorized that the random-seeming list of abominations in Leviticus offer insight into the conceptual categories of ancient Hebrew society; those things which are abominated are the ones that don't respect the categories. Whether she's right or not—and it's worth noting that Douglas herself later retracted the idea—there's definitely some truth to the underlying concept, which is that societies and individuals tend to feel unease around things that challenge or violate their mental map of the world. Julia Kristeva developed this idea to discuss horror in her theory of abjection.

One of the obvious places this shows up is with gender. Delving properly into the topic of gender will have to wait for a later volume—it's likely to eat up several essays all on its own—but for now I'll note that this can play out in a variety of ways: the bad manifestation is fear or hatred of those who violate gender norms and efforts to force them into a recognized box, while in the better manifestation a society may ascribe supernatural merit or power to the state or act of transgressing those boundaries. Shamanic traditions often make use of this, either by recruiting genderqueer people to become shamans, or by incorporating crossdressing and other such behaviors into their rituals. (In the Japanese film *Onmyōji 2*, the magician Abe no Seimei saves the world by dressing up as a Shinto shrine maiden and dancing.)

Liminality is part of why you get chimeras, using that word

in the broad sense of mythological creatures that appear to be stitched together out of pieces of different animals. (I think it also happened because if you saw or heard about an animal unfamiliar to you, sometimes the only way to describe it was to compare it to a patchwork of things you *did* recognize.) Undead monsters are liminal: neither alive nor dead, and horrifying as a result. If you want a creature in your story to feel unsettling or numinous, finding a way to place it on the boundaries between existing categories can help you do that.

That's only scratching the surface of all the different ways this permeates our storytelling, but it should be enough to give you a sense of the concept, and an eye for where it crops up in the narratives you read or watch or write.

And I think it's important to be aware of it. I said at the beginning of this post that liminality is dangerous: it exposes the categories you're using to think with, and because its effect is often disturbing, leveraging that can easily equate to treating your liminal object as horrific. My short story "The Mirror-City" is about gender and genderqueerness...which is why I backed away from using that idea for a horror anthology. It would have been incredibly easy to make it work—but then the story would have been about how genderqueerness is horrifying, and that was not a story I wanted to tell. (So instead I wrote about the liminality of time, during the transition from the Julian to the Gregorian calendar, on the night that St. Teresa of Ávila died.)

Basically: use with caution. But do use it, because its effect can be amazing.

Afterword

And that's it for the first year! As I said at the start, the New Worlds Patreon is still going strong. The plan for what I'm going to post when is continually shifting, thanks to patron requests, new ideas, and topics taking more essays to get through than I originally anticipate, but Year Two is likely to include subjects ranging from body modification to oaths, succession laws and inheritance, geoglyphs, and the always-sexy topic of sanitation. (Do you want your medieval-style city to be filthy or relatively clean? Both options are realistic!)

I want to thank all my patrons for their support, and to thank you, gentle reader, for picking up this book. It's a pleasure to be able to ramble on about these things, to remind myself of the odd little facts I've piled up in my head and add to the pile every time I go to do research for a new essay. I hope it gives you inspiration for your own work or a greater appreciation for the fiction you read—and, for that matter, a greater appreciation for the very real world we live in.

About the Author

Marie Brennan is a former anthropologist and folklorist who shamelessly pillages her academic fields for material. She is most recently misapplied her professors' hard work to the Hugo Award-nominated Victorian adventure series The Memoirs of Lady Trent; the first book of that series, *A Natural History of Dragons*, was nominated for a World Fantasy Award and won the Prix Imaginales for Best Translated Novel. "Cold-Forged Flame", the first novella in the Varekai series, came out in September 2016. She is also the author of the Doppelanger duology of Warrior and Witch, the urban fantasies *Lies and Prophecy* and *Chains and Memory*, the Onyx Court historical fantasy series, and more than fifty short stories. For more information, visit www.swantower.com.

About Book View Café

Book View Café Publishing Cooperative is an author-owned cooperative of over fifty professional writers, publishing in a variety of genres such as fantasy, romance, mystery, and science fiction.

BVC authors include *New York Times* and *USA Today* bestsellers; Nebula, Hugo, and Philip K. Dick Award winners; World Fantasy Award, Campbell Award, and RITA Award nominees; and winners and nominees of many other publishing awards.

Since its debut in 2008, BVC has gained a reputation for producing high-quality e-books, and is now bringing that same quality to its print editions.

Made in the USA
Columbia, SC
02 June 2021